AMAR
PURANA

AMAR PURANA

22 Eternal Stories from the Sacred Texts of India

PUJA RAI

JAICO PUBLISHING HOUSE

Ahmedabad Bangalore Chennai
Delhi Hyderabad Kolkata Mumbai

Published by Jaico Publishing House
A-2 Jash Chambers, 7-A Sir Phirozshah Mehta Road
Fort, Mumbai - 400 001
jaicopub@jaicobooks.com
www.jaicobooks.com

© Puja Rai

AMAR PURANA
ISBN 978-93-49358-34-8

First Jaico Impression: 2025

Page design and layout by Jojy Philip, Delhi

Printed by
Thomson Press India Limited, New Delhi

Contents

Preface

In the bustling landscape of modern life, where the complexities of ambitions, responsibilities and aspirations often drown us, we find ourselves seeking support to keep us afloat. In trying to keep ourselves balanced in the ever-demanding time of history, we can take help from the timeless wisdom of ancient scriptures to untangle the knots of life.

Among the countless narratives that populate these sacred texts, which were part of India's rich oral tradition, lie profound insights and enduring lessons that resonate deeply with the challenges and aspirations of contemporary professionals.

This book is a humble endeavor to bridge the chasm between the ancient and the contemporary, to breathe new life into age-old tales that pulsate with relevance and resonance for modern lifestyles. Within these pages lie narratives plucked from the

Vedic hymns, the mystical Upanishads, the epic sagas of the Ramayana and the Mahabharata, and the vibrant tales of the Puranas — each story a gem sparkling with profound insights and timeless truths.

Stories, as we know, are the bearers of the culture and values of a society. They are amusing as well as enlightening. Every story is a journey, and through this book, we embark on many such journeys of entertainment, enlightenment, motivation and inspiration. The luminous threads of storytelling have woven these stories such that each story retains its significance individually, and collectively, they offer profound insight into the psychological realm of life management.

In the retelling of these ancient tales, we encounter a wealth of characters and scenarios that offer a panoramic view of the human condition, inviting us to reflect on themes such as the intricacies of decision-making, pursuit of happiness, dynamics of gender and power, management of relationships, cultivation of humility, involvement in selfless service, and the acknowledgement of our inherent obligation as human beings.

As we journey through these sacred texts, we encounter a pantheon of gods and goddesses, sages and seers, heroes and heroines, whose lives are woven with threads of duty, honor, love, sacrifice, strategy, mistakes, ownership, and renunciation.

They serve as mirrors that reflect the complexities of human nature, the dilemmas of ethical conduct, and the perennial quest for meaning and fulfillment. They remind us that the challenges we face in our professional lives—whether in the boardroom or the battlefield—are not so different from those encountered by our ancient forebears.

Not all decisions are black and white; often, individuals must navigate complex choices where their duties in different roles conflict. Decision-making demands a nuanced understanding of one's duties and responsibilities across different roles as well as the cultivation of discernment (*vivek*) in distinguishing good from bad, temporary from permanent, and the visible world from the transcendent. History is replete with examples of pivotal decisions shaping the course of events. Duryodhana chose Krishna's army over Lord Krishna, Vibhishana sided with Lord Rama in the war, Sita accompanied Rama during exile, Yuyutsu joined the Pandavas against his brothers, and Karna, despite being offered an alliance with the Pandavas, aligned with Duryodhana even though he knew Duryodhana's wrongdoing.

Yet, as we grapple with the complexities of external challenges, we are also reminded to turn inward in our search for fulfillment and contentment. The tale of the musk deer, which shows the futility of chasing external sources of happiness, serves as a poignant reminder of the pointlessness of seeking contentment in the transient pleasures of the world. Instead, we are encouraged to introspect and cultivate a deeper understanding of the inner workings of the mind, recognizing that true happiness lies not in possession, but in the state of being.

On the crossroads of conflict and adversity, we find lessons of leadership, resilience, and moral courage that resonate with the trials and tribulations of contemporary professionals navigating the turbulent waters of corporate competition, societal expectations, and personal growth. Through the trials of Nala and Damayanti's relationship, the wisdom of Uddalaka in addressing his scholar son Shvetketu, the counselling of Satyabhama by Draupadi, and the compassion of Lord Rama for the *Kevat* (boatman), we gain insights into the art of decision-making, the importance of integrity, the power of perseverance, and the skill of systematic problem-solving.

Similarly, the stories of renunciants like Sulabha offer a counternarrative to prevailing stereotypes about the role of women in society, challenging us to re-examine our assumptions and prejudices. Through their courage and resilience, these women serve as beacons of hope and inspiration for those who dare to defy societal norms and carve their own path in pursuit of truth and self-realization.

Despite technological progress, our fear of the unknown persists and deepens over time. The belief in Dikpala, the guardians of the directions, symbolizes God's omniscience. The belief in guardian deities protecting the world in all directions and maintaining the order of the universe is a source of comfort for a peaceful and prosperous existence. It gives us hope that someone guards us against unseen situations and events. This belief, rooted in ancient times, soothes minds and influences attitudes, shaping the course of our lives.

Finally, amidst the vicissitudes of life, we find solace in the belief in guardian deities, whose benevolent presence provides comfort and reassurance in times of uncertainty. Whether in the form of Dikpalas guarding the directions or personal gods guiding our destinies, these stories remind us of the enduring power of faith and devotion in shaping our lives and destinies.

Storytelling has been recognised as a strong pedagogical tool in education. Indian scriptures also engaged this pedagogy to reach out to the population. The wise folks knew that stories grab attention and it is easier to retain learning through stories. There are innumerable stories in the oral and written tradition of Indian scriptures about gods and demi-gods that connect their lives to human lives for our learning, showing that nothing is permanent—a divine being can lose his position, as happened with Indra or a demon, or a thief can attain divine status, as happened with Kuber.

A few characters in these stories, significantly Chandra Dev, offer the insight that whatever has form—whether gods, humans, or animals—expresses shades of emotions, and whatever is formless—divine consciousnes or the disembodied self—is beyond emotions and feelings. This story genre is commonly found in ancient scriptures and offers guidance for people. The embodied forms of god, who display an array of emotions with which we can identify and relate, are intelligently embedded in stories that offer debates and discourses.

At the heart of these scriptural narratives lies a profound understanding of the divine, both in its manifested (*saguna*) and unmanifested (*nirguna*) forms. Whether through the anthropomorphic depictions of gods and goddesses or the abstract concepts of Brahman and *nirguna*, these stories invite us to contemplate the nature of existence and the interconnectedness of all things. They remind us that beyond the limitations of form and identity lies a boundless realm of consciousness where distinctions dissolve and the true essence of reality is revealed.

In exploring the psychological depths of the human psyche, these stories offer a road map for understanding the complexities of the mind and its various dimensions. From the principle of *ahamkara* to the intricacies of *antah karan*, we are invited to delve into the inner workings of our consciousness, confronting our egos and biases with humility and introspection.

Meaningful relationships are at the core of human life. A meaningful relationship is a universal desire, transcending culture and boundaries since antiquity. Our social and personal connections are the foundation of human civilization. Families, communities, and nations are all built on the bedrock of relationships. Through these connections, we share resources, collaborate, and create a sense of shared purpose. They are our crucial support system in navigating life's journey and are responsible for emotional fulfillment. Most characters in this book, such as Lopamudra and Agastya, Draupadi and Satyabhama, Nala and Damayanti, or Arundhati and Agastya, personify the need for a meaningful relationship. Other stories have indirect references to meaningful relationships being the foundation of all other activities.

In assembling this collection of stories, the aim is not merely to demonstrate the practical relevance of Indian scriptures but also to offer a timeless repository of wisdom and insight for generations to come. The short stories also provide an opportunity for time-strapped young professionals and students

to develop an understanding of the relevance of
these scriptural narratives. May these tales serve
as a guiding light in the darkness, illuminating
the path toward self-discovery, ethical living, and
spiritual awakening.

ॐ द्यौः शान्तिरन्तरिक्षं शान्तिः
पृथिवी शान्तिरापः शान्तिरोषधयः शान्तिः ।
वनस्पतयः शान्तिर्विश्वेदेवाः शान्तिर्ब्रह्म शान्तिः
सर्वं शान्तिः शान्तिरेव शान्तिः सा मा शान्तिरेधि ॥
ॐ शान्तिः शान्तिः शान्तिः ॥

(May peace radiate in the sky as well as in the
vast ethereal space everywhere. May peace reign all
over the earth, in water, and in all herbs, trees, and
creepers. May peace flow over the whole universe.
May peace be there in the supreme being, Brahman.
And may there always exist in all, peace and
peace alone.)

Yudhisthira trapped in a prophecy:
The search for deeper answers

Conflict often arises from a person's reluctance to act, driven by the fear that their actions may incite conflict. In attempting to avoid situations that might lead to discord, we unwittingly become caught in the trap we sought to evade. Thus, both action and inaction can be catalysts for conflict.

This philosophy of conflict fits various characters in the Mahabharata and even more so in our day-to-day lives. In the epic, Yudhisthira, the eldest of the Pandavas, known for his unwavering commitment to truth and righteousness, stands as the stark opposite to his cousin, Duryodhana, the eldest of the Kauravas, who was driven by ambition and envy toward the Pandavas. At one point in this story of the rivalry between the Pandavas and the Kauravas, Yudhisthira, who is *dharma* personified, finds himself seated opposite Shakuni (Duryodhana's maternal

uncle) for a game of dice—the game that proved to
be the turning point in the Mahabharata.

Before the invitation for the dice game was sent to
the Pandavas in Hastinapur, the Kauravas had spent
quite some time at the grand Maya Sabha, a palace
of illusions built by the demon Mayasura for the
Pandavas. The palace was considered as magnificent
as Lord Indra's palace. During this time, Yudhisthira
successfully performed the Rajasuya Yagna,
attracting Kshatriyas, celestials, sages, and other
beings worldwide. On his visit to the Pandavas, Sage
Narada imparted valuable advice on kingly duties
to Yudhisthira and described the palaces of many
famous celestials like Varuna, Indra, Kubera, Yama,
and a few more.

After the Rajasuya Yagna, the guests started
taking leave individually. Intending to take leave

of the Pandavas, Sage Narada visited them in the Sabha. But before he left, the sage said something that left Yudhisthira perplexed. Narada said that as a consequence of the Rajasuya Yagna, three kinds of warnings — atmospheric, celestial, and terrestrial — would occur, and the indications of these warnings were primarily unpleasant.

Sage Narada's words instilled fear in Yudhisthira's mind. A few days later, when Maharishi Vyasa expressed the desire to take leave and travel toward Mount Kailash with his disciples, Yudhisthira sought the wisdom of the revered sage to clear his doubts.

Yudhisthira, addressing Sage Vyasa, said, "Oh, chief of men, there is a doubt in my mind, and you are the most capable of resolving it." Yudhisthira told Vyasa what Sage Narada had told him about the portents due to the Rajasuya Yagna. He asked Maharishi Vyasa whether the unpleasant events had ended with the death of the Chedi king, Shishupala.

Ved Vyasa, rather than affirming that the unpleasant events had ended with the death of Shishupala, stated that the worst was yet to come. He told Yudhisthira that 13 years later, the portents would bear mighty consequences, ending up in the destruction of all the Kshatriyas in the world. Vyasa further said that in due course, Yudhisthira would be made the sole cause for the end of all the Kshatriyas who had assembled for the Rajasuya Yagna.

Yudhisthira was alarmed by these words. He had approached Maharishi Vyasa with the hope that he would affirm his belief that the death of the Chedi king was the unpleasant portent that Sage Narada had referred to. However, instead of confirming Yudhisthira's thoughts, Vyasa had added to Narada's statement by saying that Yudhisthira would become the cause of the end of all the famous Kshatriyas who had assembled for the *yagna*.

Overwhelmed with despair and grief, Yudhisthira considered it better to die than be the cause of such calamity. Upon seeing his brother so vulnerable, Arjuna reassured him and encouraged him to act with reason.

Then, mustering courage and thinking deeply, Yudhisthira made a resolution for the upcoming 13 years. "I shall not speak a harsh word to any of my brothers, fellow kings, or relatives," he resolved. "Living under the command of my relatives, I shall practice virtue exemplifying my vows."

He thought that if he continued to live in this way, making no distinction between his family and others, there would be no disagreement between him and others. Yudhisthira believed that disagreement was the cause of war in this world. So, doing what is agreeable to everyone would help him keep war at a distance, and he would be free from the Maharishi's prophecy of becoming the cause of the

Kshatriyas' destruction. Yudhisthira thus vowed not to speak harshly to anyone, treating his children and others equally to avoid disagreements that might lead to war.

The Pandavas bid farewell to the guests who had come for the Rajasuya Yagna. However, Duryodhana and the Kuru princes, along with Shakuni, remained at the Palace of Illusions. Duryodhana's jealousy grew as he watched the prosperity of the Pandavas. His heart burned with a desire to possess their wealth and happiness.

Even after returning, he looked cheerless and sad. Shakuni, his maternal uncle, saw an opportunity and proposed the evil solution of the fateful game of dice to fulfill Duryodhana's sinister plans. Duryodhana knew that his uncle was a skilful dice player and Yudhisthira would lose. So, winning was sure, but the difficult part was convincing Dhritarashtra and the other seniors to permit the unethical game with the Pandavas. Despite the objections of wise counsel like Bhishma, Vidura, and Drona, King Dhritarashtra succumbed to his son's wicked ambitions because of his extreme affection for his son. He permitted the unfortunate game of dice between the Pandavas and the Kauravas.

The invitation was sent to the Pandavas. Yudhisthira, with the foreknowledge of Vyasa's prophecy, was aware that his current actions might create a situation for war in 13 years. Since his actions could potentially trigger the downfall of the formidable Kshatriyas gathered for the Rajasuya Yagna, he thought it was wise to do what pleased others. Understanding that declining Duryodhana's invitation would mean disagreements, Yudhisthira accepted, participating in a game that was not recommended for wise Kshatriyas.

The invitation and acceptance to the game of dice marked the beginning of the war prophesied by Vyasa, signaling the end of the Kaurava clan. Yudhisthira, bound by his vow to avoid disagreement and keep the Kauravas content, reluctantly participated in the unethical game despite knowing that it was rigged.

The paradox surrounding Yudhisthira's decision to participate in the game of dice with Duryodhana raises numerous questions. As the embodiment of truth and justice, why did Yudhisthira yield to Duryodhana's request? He possessed the wisdom to discern the evil nature of the game, and he had influential figures like Drona, Bhishma, and Vidura who would have supported him, had he chosen to refuse. He knew the game was evil. Why did he not seek the counsel of his brothers and his wife?

In the modern world, criticism mounts regarding Yudhisthira's decision to stake his brothers and Draupadi without their consent. Did he consult them before placing Draupadi at risk? What about

Draupadi's autonomy in deciding her fate? Did Yudhisthira's commitment to righteousness and *dharma* not deter him from endangering the palace, treasury, and the welfare of the kingdom's people?

As rightly said, uneasy lies the head that wears the crown, so we are obliged to comprehend Yudhisthira's perspective. He was revered by people, celestial beings, gods, and sages as the embodiment of *dharma* and justice. Yudhisthira's character is marked by his compassion and selflessness, which is evident in various situations where he tried to alleviate others' suffering even in his own adversity.

Yet, paradoxically, his decisions ultimately contributed to one of history's most devastating wars, resulting in immense loss of life and the downfall of mighty Kshatriya rulers. Even a mighty king, the epitome of *dharma*, could not escape the trap of prophecy.

In delving into Yudhisthira's psyche, we confront the complexities of moral decision-making and the weight of leadership responsibilities. Yudhisthira's journey reminds us that even the most virtuous and mighty individuals face complexities in situations when they have to decide for others. Many a time the ease of making decisions for oneself often contrasts sharply with the difficulty of making decisions on behalf of others. Yudhisthira's situation reminds us to consider the importance of seeking counsel, honoring autonomy, and weighing the consequences of our decisions for others. The story exposes us to the subtle reality that even the pursuit of righteousness can have unintended and far-reaching consequences.

According to the Bhagavad Gita, "You have the right to perform your duties, but you do not have the right to the fruits of your action. Do not get attached to the fruits of your action or seek to choose inaction." (The Bhagavad Gita, 2.47)

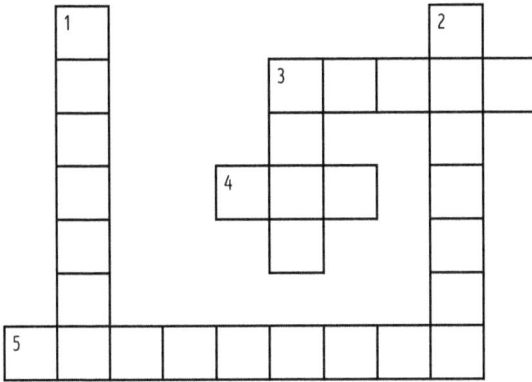

ACROSS

3 Brother of Dhritarashtra and Pandu

4 The number of years for Pandavas to stay in disguise (*agyatvaas*) after they lost the dice game

5 Stepmother of Bhishma Pitamah

DOWN

1 Guru Bhakt Aruni was the disciple of this famous rishi

2 Whose marriage with Krishna was the cause of enmity between Shishupala and Krishna?

3 The Parva of the Mahabharata that describes the forest exile period of the Pandavas

2

Tomorrow is another day:
Yuyutsu rose to *dharma*

Life gives us choices, and our wisdom and steadfastness to values help us select our preferences.
Every day we make choices, some of which
significantly impact our life while others marginally
affect a few moments of pleasure and pain. Our choices
have the power to define who we are; hence, they must
be guided by our values and beliefs with optimism.

History is full of stories where the future course
of action depended primarily on the choices made
by the person in question. Duryodhana chose
Lord Krishna's army over Lord Krishna himself.
Vibhishana decided to desert his brother and support
Lord Rama in the war. Sita chose to join her husband
Rama in the 14 years of *vanvaas*. Vasudeva (another
name of Lord Krishna) asked Karna to join the
Pandavas' side as they were brothers from the same
mother, but Karna opted for Duryodhana's side even

though he was aware that Duryodhana was wrong. Similarly, Yuyutsu, Duryodhana's stepbrother, chose the Pandavas' side in the war against his brothers.

Yuyutsu, though a lesser-known character in the Mahabharata, holds a significant place in the epic because of the circumstances surrounding his birth and his survival during the battle of Kurukshetra where all the Kuru princes were killed. Yuyutsu's birth was out of the desperation and anxiety of Dhritarashtra, the blind Kuru king. Since Queen Gandhari's gestation period was unusually long, Dhritarashtra chose to have a child through Sugadha, Gandhari's maid, because he was desperate for an heir. Thus, Yuyutsu was born, and after his birth came the birth of Duryodhana and the other Kauravas.

Yuyutsu was not only a moral warrior, but he was also a strong on-field warrior believed to possess the powers to fight 60,000 warriors alone. He was considered an *atirathi*. An *atirathi* is a warrior who is equivalent to 12 *rathis*. Yuyutsu was also instrumental in saving Bhima's life as he shared the information about how Duryodhana was planning to poison the water that Bhima was to drink.

Yuyutsu was the one Kaurava prince who was alive after the Kurukshetra war as he made the right decision at the right time, choosing to side with righteousness and *dharma* rather than his blood relations.

It is a paradox in the story of the Mahabharata that despite the presence of ethically and morally principled seniors and gurus like Bhishma, Drona, Vidura, Kripacharya, and Vyasa, the Kurukshetra war could not be avoided. Further, the value system in which Bhishma and Drona believed was akin to that of Yudhisthira, but they still fought against Yudhisthira and the Pandava army.

Bhishma Pitamah, Dronacharya, and Vidura's minds and hearts belonged to the Pandavas, but they devoted their physical bodies as warriors to the Kauravas. Though they were the lead warriors of the Kaurava side, they did not believe in Duryodhana or the Kauravas' righteousness, but they still had to fight in their favor. This non-belongingness of the warriors to their team was a strategic factor for the Kauravas losing the war. Our decisions and actions must be in harmony with our values and beliefs. If we are forced to act against our deep-rooted values by situational compulsions, we go into total disharmony within ourselves. Bhishma Pitamah, Dronacharya, Kripacharya, and Shalya (the Pandavas' maternal uncle) could not muster the moral courage to go to the Pandavas' side for the war as their words bound them. Yuyutsu, for whom *dharma* was more valuable than social obligations, crossed the boundary and went to the Pandavas' side. He wanted to end his internal disharmony.

At the beginning of the Kurukshetra war, when both armies were standing opposite each other with their strategic array of foot soldiers and horse- and elephant-mounted warriors, Yudhisthira, the eldest of the Pandavas, approached their great-grandfather, Bhishma, and sought his blessing. Bhishma blessed him with success in the war and accepted that he was not free and was bound to the Kauravas' side.

Yudhisthira then asked Bhishma Pitamah how he could be defeated, to which Bhishma replied that no one in this world could beat him. Bhishma once again blessed Yudhisthira with success in the war.

After that, Yudhisthira approached Guru Dronacharya. He sought his guru's blessing and asked the invincible warrior how the Pandavas could fight so that they defeat all their foes without incurring any sin. Dronacharya, happy with the

complete surrender and respect from Yudhisthira, felt gratified and said he was no longer a free man. He was under the obligation of the wealth of the Kauravas and had to be on their side. He said that he would fight for the Kauravas but would pray for the success of the Pandavas.

Next, Yudhisthira approached Kripacharya and stood in silence for some time. Kripa (Gautama), knowing his intentions, told Yudhisthira that he was incapable of being slain but advised him to fight and prayed for his victory.

After this, he paid his respects to Shalya and got blessings from him. Shalya also expressed his inability to help the Pandavas but blessed Yudhisthira to be a winner. Meanwhile, Vasudeva proposed to Karna to join the Pandavas, as they were brothers. Karna refused to leave Duryodhana as he was devoted to whatever was agreeable to Dhritarashtra's son.

Finally, Yudhisthira placed himself at the center of the warring groups on the battlefield and announced that whoever wanted to join them could do so, and the Pandavas would forever protect them and become their ally. Hearing these words, Yuyutsu, the stepbrother of the Kauravas, chose to side with the Pandavas. Yuyutsu was welcomed by Vasudeva and the Pandavas. Yudhisthira, like a confident warrior, happily received Yuyutsu and made an impactful statement for both sides.

"Yuyutsu, with this decision of yours, you will save Dhritarashtra's lineage."

These words of Yudhisthira guaranteed the outcome of the war, indicating the saving of *dharma* and the annihilation of *adharma* and the Kaurava lineage simultaneously.

Yuyutsu rose to *dharma* at the brink of the war. He valued the *dharma* for which the Pandavas were fighting and believed in the value of justice. He knew that injustice was meted out to the Pandavas, and he needed to stand with them. Making some decisions often requires courage to break free from old, forced decisions. Yuyutsu, by choosing the Pandavas' side, also ended the internal disharmony between his value, which were with the Pandavas, and his social situation, which had placed him with the Kauravas. Though he believed in the righteousness and *dharma* of the Pandavas, being the stepbrother of the Kauravas, he was on their side by design.

The story of a lesser-known character in the Mahabharata who chose the right path at the right moment is worth sharing and pondering. One's decision should be in harmony with one's belief system and values. The story of Yuyutsu shows his determination to resolve the dilemma between his decision and his values and deciding in favor of *dharma* just when it was desired.

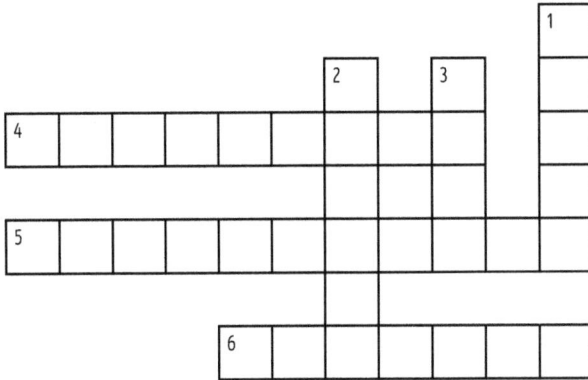

ACROSS

4 Another name for Bhishma Pitamah

5 Name given to Krishna's conch

6 Son of Dhritarashtra and Sugadha

DOWN

1 The acharya who was a great archer and teacher of both the Pandavas and the Kauravas. He was adopted by King Shantanu as an infant

2 Dhritarashtra's charioteer who had the gift of seeing things at long distance

3 Kunti's son and the Pandavas' half-brother who fought on the Kauravas' side in the Kurukshetra war

Untangling happiness:
Yajnavalkya and Maitreyi

The search for happiness is a universal human desire that reflects our innate need for meaning and purpose in life. While happiness can be elusive and difficult to define, it remains a powerful force that drives us to seek joy, fulfillment, and a sense of connection.

Pursuing happiness has been one of the most sought-after desires throughout history. It is the most fundamental desire for humans as it is associated with a sense of well-being and is also a measure of success. With the affordability and wide reach of digital technology, social media has replaced our natural world. Social media has created a buzz around happiness; people are pressured to be happy or look happy. However, this pressure to conform to the societal pressure of looking happy created by social media, advertising, and the popular culture of immediate gratification has made people unhappier than ever before.

The world's most developed nations are contemplating making happiness a policy subject. This also makes us realize that material prosperity and happiness are not directly proportional. Money or material possessions can bring a sense of well-being but not happiness.

Throughout history, thinkers have pondered the nature of happiness, but the search continues, similar to the pursuit of a musk deer, who was looking for the fragrance that accompanied it since it was born. While all other musk deers of its age played and enjoyed themselves, this deer restlessly searched, all its life, for the source of the familiar fragrance since its birth.

Anxious, the deer left its family and traveled far and wide alone, but all the efforts were in vain. One day, out of frustration, it decided to end its life by jumping into a well. However, a sage saw the deer and asked why it looked sad. The deer described the pain of his life. The sage laughed at the deer and said, "You don't need to jump in the well for your search, but rather, look at your reflection in the water. You will get the answer. The fragrance is within you."

We humans, too, often pursue happiness through external means, overlooking the intrinsic nature of joy. This narrative perpetuates the illusion that happiness is linked to material objects, ignoring the transient nature of external attachments and the enduring source of joy within oneself.

An incident from the Brihadaranyaka Upanishad and a discussion between Sage Yajnavalkya and his wife, Maitreyi, offers further insight into this conflict of life. The learned Sage Yajnavalkya had two wives, Maitreyi and Katyayani. When it was the appropriate time to renounce the social and family life according to the rules of ashram dharma, Sage Yajnavalkya informed and sought permission from both his wives. He said, "It is the right time for me to renounce the world. I will divide my material possessions equally so you can spend the rest of your life comfortably." Katyayani, a simple lady, accepted the proposal as this was the norm of the society at that time. But Maitreyi had a few questions

about his proposal. She asked the sage if the material possessions he left for her would make her happy and immortal. The sage replied that these material possessions would neither make her happy nor immortal. Maitreyi then wonders what she would do with these valuable possessions if they couldn't make her happy or immortal.

Yajnavalkya explains that these material possessions are temporal, and so is the feeling of happiness on acquiring them. Material possessions could give her comfort in life but could not make her happy.

We feel happy when we possess, own, or achieve certain things because of an altered state of mind on acquiring or possessing the object that our Self desires. No actual physical connection between the object and the mind happens outside the mind. So, it is our Self that defines the relationship, and it is for the happiness of our Self that we attach value to external objects. Nothing is dear in this world on its own. What is dear is the condition that our Self intends to create or project in our mind by an imagined contact with the object. So, a person is not special to us, but what is dear is the condition imagined to be present from possessing that object or relationship.

Yajnavalkya goes on with his exposition to Maitreyi: "Neither the husband is dear to the wife, nor the wife is dear to the husband. What is dear is a condition they try to bring about in their mind from that relationship. That condition, if not achieved, will not lead to the expected happiness. A wife loves her husband not because the husband independently has a value of happiness attached to him, but because the wife's mind has perceived that imaginary value. The husband doesn't love the wife for the wife's sake but to make himself happy." Suppose the husband (as an external object) independently carries the value of happiness within himself. In that case, the husband's presence should always lead to the exact condition of joy for the wife. But we know that is not true, as is the case when couples get divorced and say they no longer feel love and happiness with each other. So, love was the state of mind as a response to the specific condition of the mind. Yajnavalkya explains this further by giving more examples.

Yajnavalkya said: "As a matter of fact, it is not for the sake of the husband, my dear, is the husband loved, but he is loved for the sake of one's own Self which, in its true nature, is one with the Supreme Self. Undoubtedly, not for the wife's sake, my dear, is the wife loved, but she is loved for the sake of the husband's Self. Verily, not for the sons' sake, my dear, are the sons loved, but they are loved for the sake of their own Self. Realistically, not for the sake of wealth, my dear, is wealth loved, but for the sake of the Self. Not for the sake of the Brahmin is the Brahmin loved, but he is loved for the sake of their own Self. Truly, not for the sake of the Kshatriya, my dear, is he loved, but for the sake of their own Self. Verily, not for the sake of the worlds, my dear, are they loved, but for the sake of the Self. Verily, not for the sake of the gods, my dear, are the gods loved, but they are loved for the sake of our own Self. Verily, not for the sake of the beings, my dear, are they loved, but for the sake of the Self. Verily, not for the sake of All, my dear, are All loved, but they are valued for the sake of the Self. In reality, my dear Maitreyi, it is the Self that should be realized—should be heard of, reflected on, and meditated upon. By the realization of the Self, my dear—through hearing, reflection and meditation—all this is known."

आत्मनस्तुकामायसर्वंप्रियंभवति, meaning, everything else becomes dear or desirable for the sake of the Self. This line sums up the long discussion between Sage Yajnavalkya and Maitreyi. Hence, the wise and learned say that happiness is a state of mind and can be achieved by practice.

The feeling of happiness from owning and possessing material objects is temporal, not eternal, as possession is not permanent, and the condition created by our mind is wavering. So, things and people are not dear to us; they are precious because our mind has been conditioned to their presence as happiness.

Hindu philosophy distinguishes between various

kinds of happiness to further clarify the confusion. We have different ways to express them. *Ananda* is the state of mind achieved by yogic practices and meditation, following any one path of *karma marga, bhakti marga,* or *jnana marga*. *Ananda* is the happiness that is not dependent on material possessions. It does not increase or decrease with an increase or decrease in material wealth.

Material possessions provide us with the comforts of life, commonly called *sukh*. So, the standard Hindi terms like *sukh, samriddhi* or prosperity, and *saubhagya* or good fortune are about material possessions. However, *ananda* or *param ananda* is a permanent happy condition of mind.

Sukh is more akin to sensual or material pleasure, but *ananda* is the mental state adopted after practice and isn't affected by the increase or decrease of material possessions. *Dukh* (sadness or grief) will always accompany *sukh*, but *ananda* is a permanent state of happiness and bliss. Vedanta talks about ways to achieve *ananda*. Even Brahman, or the divine consciousness, is defined as *sat, chit,* and *ananda*.

Happiness or *ananda* is the state that can be achieved when we are not narrow and limited. So, the more we attach happiness to our Self's desire, the shorter it will last — the more holistic and broader our approach to life, the more prolonged the happiness. There is no happiness in a fragmented life. The more we identify our lives with others and understand that we all are part of that bigger reality, the nearer we move to the state of *ananda*. Differentiation is the cause of sorrow, so we must aim to achieve a state of self-sameness with all beings — this is the path to happiness.

Happiness is the state beyond duality.

Happiness is characteristic of Brahman, so it is *purna* (whole) and not fragmented. It is interdependent. It is not a standalone element. Belief and practice of self-sameness will lead to the realization of the philosophy of interdependence. Fragmentation is not the nature of happiness, but completeness or wholeness is.

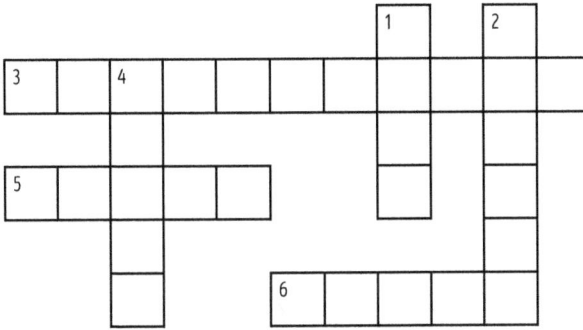

ACROSS

3 The *ashram dharma* which was a transition stage to prepare for the final renunciation and places emphasis on pursuing *moksha*

5 The *shastra* (text) that clarifies and explains the methodology of worship

6 Another famous female Veda scholar during Maitreyi's time

DOWN

1 So'hamasmi (सोऽहमस्मि), the prayer mantra meaning "I am He" or "Even when I pray to You, I am You" is from which Upanishad?

2 Manusmriti is a Smriti, whereas the Vedas are classified as _ _ _ _ _

4 The school of Indian philosophy that discusses logic and epistemology in detail

4

Pitripaksha:
Everyone has a debt to repay

Shraadh is one of the oldest and most meaningful rituals of ancestral worship or tribute to our ancestors in Hinduism. Ancestors or *pitri* hold a significant position in Hinduism. They are integral to one's existence; we derive our identity from them. It is imperative to ensure that we offer sacrifices to able Brahmins and perform rituals to repose our ancestors' souls. These rituals are said to help the ancestors' souls to migrate from *pretaloka* to *pitriloka*.

The soul, laden with karmic afflictions of worldly experiences, finds it difficult to migrate from *pretaloka* to *pitriloka*. The *shraadh* rituals during *pitripaksha* are supposed to provide them with a way to move to *pitriloka*. The concept of *pitri*, methods to gratify our ancestors and consequences of not doing so, are mentioned in nearly all the significant scriptures, including the Rigveda, the Upanishads, the Ramayana, the Mahabharata, and the Puranas.

The Rigveda mentions the ancestors and methods to gratify them. One of the *shlokas* in the Rigveda says that Agnidev is created as a *purohit* who acts as a protector of ancestors who are our protectors. With utmost reverence, we pray to Agni that he may protect us and provide us with wealth.

The Brihadaranyaka Upanishad mentions the three realms of existence or the three *lokas*: *prithviloka*, *pitriloka*, and *devaloka*. Of these, *pitriloka* can be won by performing rites.

Paying homage to ancestors is one of the oldest rituals in most religions worldwide. Despite so many changes and global cultural exposure to different religious practices and beliefs, the ritual of *shraadh* in the period of *pitripaksha* holds a significant position in the life of a practicing Hindu. While performing *shraadh*, Brahmins are revered, and food balls called *pinda* are made and offered to crows. As Hinduism is an

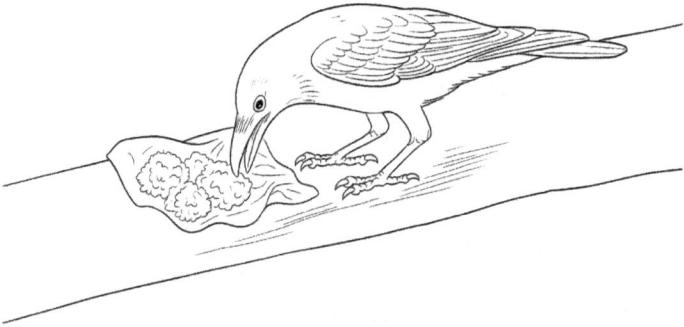

inclusive region, all living beings have their importance at specific times and in specific rituals. Crows are important during *shraadh*. Crows are considered messengers of ancestors, and some also believe them to be representative of the Lord of Death, Yama.

Shraadh is observed in *pitripaksha*, a 16-day period in the Hindu lunar calendar in the month of Bhadrapada. Bhadrapada Purnima (full moon) is the first day of *pitripaksha*, and the last day of *pitripaksha* is the Amavasya (no moon) of the succeeding Ashwin month of the Hindu calendar.

Directions (*dasha*) and time (*kaal*) have particular importance in Hindu religious practices, astronomy, astrology, and architecture. The South celestial sphere is considered the place of the ancestors in the Hindu religion. So, *pitripaksha* is observed when the sun is toward the Southern Hemisphere. The sun starts its southern journey or *dakshinayan* in June as per the Gregorian calendar.

Most of the *dakshinayan* period, particularly *pitripaksha*, is considered unfavorable for any auspicious work, as opposed to the period when the sun is *uttarayan* (toward the Northern Hemisphere), when Makar Sankranti is observed.

The ritual of *shraadh* also finds its roots in the Vedic philosophy of *rin* or debt. The tradition of *rin* or obligation (debt) is firmly embedded in the Hindu way of life. There are various stories in ancient scriptures about *rin* and the consequences of its non-repayment.

The three prominent types of *rin* in the Vedic and Upanishadic period were *pitri rin, deva rin* and *rishi rin.* Later, *manushya rin* and *bhuta rin* were added to the types of debt. The concept of *rin* in Hinduism emphasizes that individuals are part of an extensive web of relationships, without which their existence is impossible. Therefore, they owe certain obligations to these entities. The concept also focuses on the philosophy of coexistence.

Pitri rin, or our obligation toward our ancestors, is one of the most significant and cannot be ignored because we owe our existence to our parents and ancestors. Two essential practices or duties are considered necessary to repay this ancestral *rin.* The first and non-negotiable duty is the practice of *grihastha ashram* and continuation of the lineage. The second is the annual tribute and worship of the ancestors through offering *shraadh* during *pitripaksha.* This yearly observance reiterates that we have a debt toward our ancestors since we exist in this world because of them. We derive our social identity from them, and their *karma* also affects us. Our ancestors have contributed to making our life easy in this world. So, we must repay them by easing their transmigration into the other world and continuing their lineage.

No one is excused from this *rin*, and they are obliged to repay it. According to a legend from the Mahabharata, even Lord Surya and Princess Kunti's son, Karna, wasn't forgiven for the non-repayment of *pitri rin*. It is said that Karna did not observe the *shraadh* ritual for his ancestors when he was on *prithvi* (Earth), so his ancestors were stuck in *pretaloka*. After his death, Karna reached *swarga* (heaven) as he had accrued merit through his charity. Upon reaching heaven, he felt hungry. However, he could not eat anything because whatever he touched turned to gold. When he inquired about this, Yama informed him that when on Earth, Karna had never offered food in the name of his ancestors.

Karna was known as *danaveer* (philanthropist) since he was involved in *daana* (charity) every day. He never let any person go empty-handed from his doorstep. Even though he knew that his *kavach* (shield) and *kundal* (earrings) made him invincible, he still gifted them to Lord Indra when Indra asked for them. He acquired immense merits from his philanthropy, but he never offered food in the name of his ancestors, nor did he perform the *shraadh* rituals. His ancestors could not get the merits of his *shraadh* and were stuck in *pretaloka*, and since his ancestors were not happy, he was experiencing this discomfort in heaven.

So, Yama allowed Karna to return to Earth for 15

days and complete the rituals of *shraadh*. Many believe that the 15-day period when Karna visited Earth to perform the rituals marks the period of *pitripaksha*. Sarvapitri Amavasya is the most important day of *pitripaksha*, where *shraadh* rituals can be offered to all irrespective of the lunar day on which they left their earthly body for their heavenly abode. Sarvapitri Amavasya, also known as Mahalya Amavasya, is the last day of *pitripaksha*.

Gaya in Bihar holds a special significance for *shraadh* rituals. Performing a *shraadh* ritual for one's ancestors in Gaya is believed to have enormous benefits for departed souls. It is suggested that every Hindu must at least once perform the *shraadh* of their ancestors in Gaya. It is believed that Lord Rama performed the *shraadh* of his father, King Dasharatha, at Gaya. Furthermore, Lord Vishnu's footmarks still exist in Gaya, where he trampled the demon Gayasur under his feet (now within the premises of Vishnupad Temple).

According to another belief, the demon Gayasur had a boon that whoever visits him shall attain *moksha* (salvation), and Gayasur would be as famous as Lord Brahma, Lord Vishnu, and Lord Shiva, which made the process of *shraadh* at Gaya significant. Apart from Gaya, other places famous for the *shraadh* ritual include Pushkar (Rajasthan), Allahabad, Kashi or Banaras, Mathura (Uttar Pradesh), Haridwar

(Uttarakhand), Kurukshetra (Haryana), and Jagannath Puri (Odisha).

At the societal and individual levels, religion and rituals provide psychological comfort and are a constant source of hope. Religion and religious practices have an equalizing effect on people. The mass event of the *shraadh* rituals at Gaya and the observance of *pitripaksha* by people from most regions of India, irrespective of economic and social status, has a calming effect. It provides psychological solace to mourning people and families — that they are not alone in the mourning process and that no person or family is untouched by the truths of life and death.

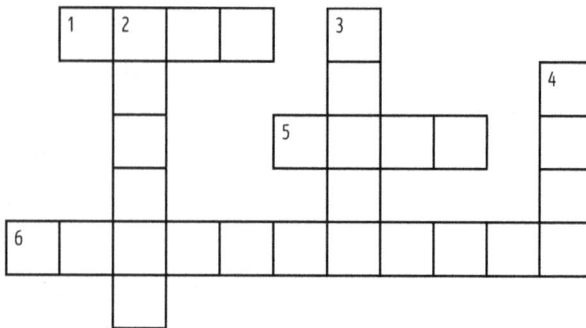

ACROSS

1 One of the gatekeepers of Vaikuntha
5 This bird is believed to be the messenger of our ancestors
6 The annual period when *shraadh* is performed for our ancestors

DOWN

2 What is the Hindu lunar calendar system in which the lunar month ends with *amavasya* called?
3 Yamaraj's father
4 One of the important centers of *shraadh* in India

The woman who lit her lamp:
The dialogue between Janak and Sulabha

The status of women in Hinduism has evolved, from periods of liberation to subjugation and partial autonomy. Throughout these phases, a prevailing belief in society is that women embody goddesses like Kali, Durga, or Lakshmi. In many regions, young girls are worshipped as manifestations of the goddess Durga, and married women are revered as symbols of Lakshmi and Annapurna. This acknowledgement of female divinity underscores Hindu rituals and traditions. In the contemporary world, women are asserting themselves, challenging societal norms, and redefining their roles beyond traditional stereotypes of marriage and motherhood. This resurgence prompts a reevaluation of ancient beliefs and a recognition of women's right to autonomy and choice in modern society.

In the Shanti Parva of the Mahabharata, Bhishma Pitamah gives various discourses while lying on the bed of arrows in the battlefield, waiting for the right time to leave his earthly body. When Yudhisthira asks him a question about the possibility of attaining emancipation while living a householder's life, Bhishma narrates the story of King Janak.

The ruler of Mithila, Janak, was known for being conversant with the Vedas and following the rules of governance while staying detached from worldly deviations. He had grown above the feeling of love for his family or hatred for his enemy. He epitomized a renunciant who was a practicing king and a householder.

In this period, there lived a woman named Sulabha, a renunciant and a *yogini* who wandered around the earth. She heard about King Janak, who was emancipated even as a king and a householder. Desirous of meeting Janak in person and interviewing him, she assumed the form of a young, beautiful woman by her yogic powers and presented herself in the court of King Janak.

Seeing a young woman of unrivaled beauty in the guise of a saint, Janak offered her a seat respectfully and was curious to know about her. He asked her who she was, where she had come from, and what she wanted. Gratified by the hospitality offered to her, Sulabha mentioned that she wanted to know about the dharma of liberation or emancipation that the king had achieved.

Sulabha, the *yogini*, used the powers of her yogic practice to enter King Janak's subtle mind. Janak, incapable of hiding his pride on being recognized as a practitioner of emancipation, suddenly experienced the presence of a foreign element in his mind. The entire debate between them took place inside their minds.

Janak asked Sulabha why she needed to enter his mind to check whether he was emancipated. He asked her where she had come from and where she would go after achieving her purpose.

He added that he was the disciple of the famous Sage Panchashikha and belonged to the Parasara race. He claimed he had control over his senses like a practicing renunciant and did not feel love for his family or hatred for his enemy. He was liberated, and at the same time, he acted like a king. For him, a

pot of clay and that of gold had the same value.

He claimed that he was well versed in the Vedas and followed the rules for a ruler. He stated that he was well versed in the philosophies of Sankhya and yoga as well. He knew that if a *sanyasi* carried aversion, anger, and attachment within himself, he was not liberated. In contrast, if a householder shunned these emotions and was in absolute control of his senses, he was emancipated. One attains emancipation by knowledge alone, and Janak claimed that though he was involved in the responsibilities of religion, kingdom, and family, he still possessed the proper knowledge through his study of the Vedas.

Janak further said that Sulabha's behavior did not correspond to the mode of life she had adopted. He said, "You have made an illegal union with me by entering my mind. The association of a Brahmin with a Kshatriya is not correct. Whether you are single or married, this unsolicited union amounts to sin. According to dharma, appearing in disguise before a Brahmin, a king, or one's wife is a sin. You have appeared in disguise before a king, which is another sin."

Janak further said that even though she was a *rishika*, Sulabha had no control over her desires, which took away all her merits.

After Janak spoke at length about his emancipation and how Sulabha had committed a sin by questioning him, it was Sulabha's turn in the debate.

Sulabha, unaffected by the king's words, challenged his understanding of the Vedas. She told Janak if he were genuinely exposed to the philosophy of non-duality, then the questions posed to Sulabha about her identity, purpose, and background would become insignificant.

Sulabha said that a king could not be independent or free. A king depended on his council of ministers for suggestions to govern and strategize against his enemies, and a good king needed to have love and affection for his subjects, which was why kings undertook welfare activities.

Sulabha challenged Janak's claims of being emancipated, stating that caste, race, or gender would not bind him if he were truly emancipated. When he questioned the union (which is also doubtful) of a Brahmin with a Kshatriya, Janak was still bound by material divisions and differences, showing that he had not understood the essence of the Vedas. Sulabha stated that an emancipated person does not see differences in color, *varna*, *gotra*, or gender, and one who is divided in all these differentiations cannot be liberated.

Sulabha told Janak that he had exposed his belief in caste stereotypes by assuming that she belonged to the Brahmin *varna* (caste), whereas she was born in a Kshatriya family. Since he believed that only a

person belonging to the Brahmin *varna* could learn
the Vedas or practice renunciation, this limitation
of thought was proof that King Janak was not
emancipated. An emancipated person does not see
these differences.

Janak had questioned the union of Sulabha and
himself and called it wrong and illicit. Rebutting this
claim, Sulabha says, "If you claim to have practiced
the philosophy of the Vedas, then how do you
question this union? When I do not belong to my
body, and when my body is not my identity, there
is no union. What harm has been done to you if I
entered your intellect? I did not touch your physical
body. Only those who consider soul and body to be
one can call this act of mine a union of two opposite
genders." After listening to Sulabha's logical debate,
Janak accepted that he still had a long way to go to
reach the stage of emancipation.

Sulabha, a *rishika*, belonged to a Kshatriya
family and did not get married since there was no
compatible match for her, and she had the freedom
to decide. She decided to acquire the knowledge of
the Vedas. Seers and knowledge seekers held her in
great esteem. She was not known to belong to any
cult or order and did not depend on any relation,
guru, or social group to derive her identity.

The   Janak–Sulabha   debate   indicates   that
the struggles of women achievers to establish

themselves and get accepted have always existed; in some phases of history, it was relatively easy, and sometimes, it was not as easy. However, these struggles are not new for us as a nation, as the ancient Indian scriptures demonstrate. At the start of the debate, Sulabha was ridiculed by Janak for trying to examine his scriptural knowledge and practices. In contrast, at the end of the discussion, there was acceptance and respect for Sulabha. Thus, gender stereotypes have always existed in society in some form, but what is significant is that Indian scriptures have numerous examples where these stereotypes were challenged and the rebuttal accepted by a knowledgeable audience.

It is a pleasant surprise for champions of gender equality to be exposed to Vedic texts, which had a very progressive way of addressing women. Vedic terms like Aditi, Sumangali, Mena, Subudha, and Visruta expressed women as independent, auspicious, deserving of respect, knowledgeable, and learned. In ancient Hindu scriptures, there are examples of female *rishikas*, teachers, goddesses, and homemakers. There is a respectable history of women assuming unconventional roles in Hinduism, and Sulabha is one example of a woman who made such choices. In the modern world, honoring women means honoring their freedom to choose and giving them equality of opportunity.

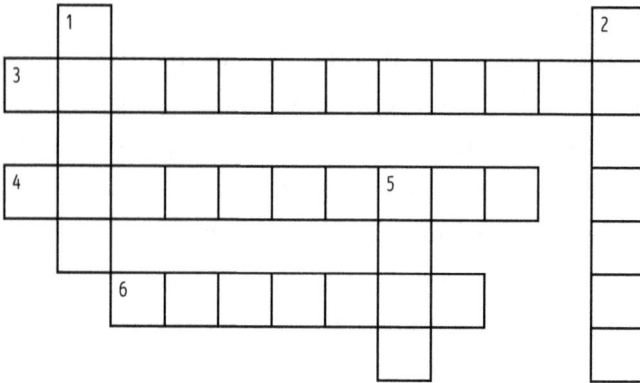

ACROSS

3 Janak's guru
4 Popular or common name of Manav Dharma Shastra
6 The rishika who won in a philosophical debate with King Janak

DOWN

1 Ruler of Mithila
2 The school of Indian philosophy that introduced the concept of the world being the interplay of *purusha* and *prakriti*
5 The other prominent Upanishad, along with the Brihadaranyaka Upanishad, that is associated with the Yajurveda

6

Akshay Patra:
Redefining our *patra* of values

In Hinduism, the act of giving, known as *daan,* is not merely a religious duty but also a source of immense joy and fulfillment. It is a way of fulfilling one's obligation toward society and all living beings. The joy of giving permeates every aspect of Hindu life, with numerous rituals and auspicious days dedicated to acts of charity.

Daan is revered for its intrinsic value, reflecting the generosity and selflessness inherent in the giver. Hindu scriptures emphasize that giving is not just about material offerings; it is also a spiritual practice that enriches both the giver and the recipient. The Bhagavad Gita expounds on three types of giving, the best being the virtues of selfless charity (*sattvikam daan*) that brings benefits beyond measure.

According to ancient texts like the Brihadaranyaka Upanishad and the Chandogya Upanishad, charity (*daan*) is among the fundamental qualities of a virtuous individual, alongside such qualities as self-restraint, compassion, and truthfulness. These teachings underscore the integral role of giving in leading a righteous and fulfilled life.

However, the essence of true giving lies in its spontaneity and selflessness. As the saying goes, "Highest form of charity is self-motivated, which is given personally by the donor by reaching out to the receiver; giving the charity by calling the receiver to take the donation is of medium grade; giving after being asked or requested is inferior in merit; and giving in exchange for services rendered is fruitless."

This statement highlights the distinction between genuine acts of charity and mere transactions, emphasizing the importance of giving with an open heart and without expectation of return.

The story of granting Akshay Patra by Lord Surya to Dharmaraj Yudhisthira is one such narrative that subtly communicates this fantastic human value of benevolence and placing others before one's self, which is to be practiced even when the giver is facing hardships in life.

In the Mahabharata, when the Pandavas had lost everything in the dice game that Yudhisthira played with Shakuni on behalf of Duryodhana, the Pandavas were left with nothing. Per the game conditions, the Pandavas were banished to the jungle for 13 years—12 years of dwelling in the forest and the last year of staying in disguise.

When Yudhisthira and the other Pandavas, along with their wife, Draupadi, started for the forest, several citizens and Brahmins followed them to show their love and respect for the Pandavas. After some time, many of the citizens stopped following them and bid their beloved king and his family farewell with heavy hearts. However, several Brahmins and their families followed the Pandavas for the next day and night.

Yudhisthira stopped and addressed them respectfully and requested them to return to the kingdom. He told them that since he had lost everything to the Kauravas, he had no resources to fulfill his *dharma* as a Kshatriya and feed the Brahmins. The Brahmins, however, were adamant about not leaving the righteous Pandavas alone and assured Yudhisthira that all they needed was space in his heart. They said that they would take care of themselves, and Yudhisthira need not bother about feeding them.

Already accused of causing hardships for his brothers and Draupadi, Yudhisthira broke down under the weight of his guilt because he could not alleviate the Brahmins' suffering.

Abandoning the Brahmins was immoral for the Pandavas, and patronizing learned Brahmins was one of the revered values of that time.

One of the enlightened Brahmins, Rishi Saunaka, approached Yudhisthira and suggested that he consult his spiritual guru, Rishi Dhaumya. Rishi Saunaka assured Yudhisthira that Rishi Dhaumya would invariably provide a solution.

Yudhisthira then sought the advice of Rishi Dhaumya, who suggested that Yudhisthira must worship the source of all life in this world, the supreme source and sustainer of all the food in this world: Lord Surya or the Sun God.

Standing in the waters of the pure Ganga and sustaining himself only on air, Yudhisthira

underwent deep penance to please Surya. Pleased by Yudhisthira's penance, Surya appeared and bestowed Yudhisthira with a copper vessel, Akshay Patra, which would provide inexhaustible food for each day. However, there was a condition for its usage. Each day, after Draupadi had taken her meal, the food would be exhausted for that day.

Thus, the Sun God granted him the boon that the Akshay (inexhaustible) Patra (vessel) would take care of their stay in the jungle and gave his blessings that the Pandavas would regain their kingdom after completing the thirteenth year of exile.

Having been granted this boon by Lord Surya, Yudhisthira was at peace and cared for the learned Brahmins and other visitors in the jungle. Every day, the Brahmins and other visitors were fed, and then the four Pandava brothers, followed by Yudhisthira and Draupadi, would consume food. However, trials and tribulations are part of human life, whether for a king or a beggar. Yudhisthira and the other Pandavas, too, soon faced a challenging situation arising from Duryodhana's deceitfulness.

Feeling threatened by the Pandavas and not being at peace even after sending them to the forest, Duryodhana convinced Rishi Durvasa to visit the Pandavas. He planned the trip such that Rishi Durvasa and his disciples would reach toward the end of the day. Duryodhana was well aware that the Pandavas and Panchali (another name for Draupadi) might be unable to welcome and feed Rishi Durvasa at that time since the Akshay Patra would not provide any more food for the day after Draupadi had finished her meal. So, as planned by Duryodhana, Rishi Durvasa and his disciples visited the Pandavas in the jungle. By the time they reached the Pandavas' abode, it was late, and the Brahmins and visitors, followed by the Pandavas and Draupadi, had finished their meal. The Akshay Patra was exhausted for the day.

Sage Durvasa was famous for his mystic powers as well as his temper. The Pandavas welcomed the sage and his entourage with complete humility and requested them to freshen up in the nearby river. While Durvasa and his disciples proceeded toward the river, Yudhisthira and Panchali were under immense anxiety at the prospect of sinning by not being able to feed the sage and the fear of his ensuing wrath.

At this challenging moment, Panchali turned to Lord Krishna for help. Lord Krishna appeared before her and asked her to feed him whatever was left in the Patra as he was hungry. With a perplexed look, Panchali showed the Akshay Patra to Lord Krishna. The Lord found one grain of rice stuck at the bottom of the vessel and ate that. At that moment, Durvasa, his disciples, and the whole universe felt satiated. They had no appetite, so the sage and his disciples went back from the river without visiting the Pandavas.

There are various beliefs about the day when the Akshay Patra was given by Lord Surya and the day Lord Krishna ate from the Patra. Some believe that the day when Lord Krishna ate from the Patra, satiating the hunger of the universe, was the day of Akshay Tritiya, whereas others believe that the day Lord Surya gave the Akshay Patra to Yudhisthira was the auspicious day of Akshay Tritiya.

Other significant events are also associated with Akshay Tritiya. According to a few scriptures, it is the day when Parashuram, an incarnation of Lord Vishnu, was born, and the day marked the beginning of Treta Yuga. Some believe that Goddess Ganga descended on Earth from heaven on this day. People also offer prayers to Goddess Annapoorna, the deity of food and nourishment, on Akshay Tritya. In Jainism, the festival of Varsi Tapa is celebrated on this day to pay homage to Rishabhdev — the first Tirthankara who ended his one-year asceticism by drinking sugarcane juice.

Another popular belief is that on the day of Akshay Tritiya, Kubera, the Banker in heaven, was granted enormous wealth by worshipping Lord Shiva and was made the custodian of prosperity and wealth along with Goddess Lakshmi.

Yet another story is associated with Lord Krishna and his old childhood friend, Sudama. It is believed that Sudama visited Lord Krishna after several years on the day of Akshay Tritiya. Sudama was extremely poor and had nothing to eat. At his wife's suggestion, he visited Lord Krishna looking for some help. He carried a small portion of puffed rice as a gift for Lord Krishna. When he met Lord Krishna, Sudama was ashamed of taking a small amount of puffed rice to a friend who was a king, so he did not offer it to him. But Lord Krishna noticed the bag, asked for it, and ate the puffed rice. Sudama, overwhelmed by Krishna's love and respect, did not ask him for help and returned. When he reached his hut, however, he saw a house full of riches instead. So, this is the day when one selflessly gives to others and the Lord returns our offerings in abundance. Akshay Tritiya inspires us to engage in *daan*, charity, for its intrinsic value, and not for any end goal.

The story of Akshay Patra emphasizes the virtue of selfless charity for those in need and their dependants. Though he was in a difficult situation himself, Yudhisthira was concerned not about his needs, but about the Brahmins who depended on him. The story shows us that if we selflessly help others, God gives us back in abundance, as Lord Surya granted Yudhisthira the Akshay Patra with the blessing that he would get back his kingdom after the exile.

Daan or charity is the most effective virtue to reduce the disharmony arising from inequality, exploitation (of people and ecology), and natural calamities. It has been eulogized in numerous Indian scriptures and institutionalized in nearly all the religions that originated in India.

Jainism talks about chaturvidha (four types) of charity: *anna daan* (giving food in charity), *aushadha daan* (giving medicines or health services in charity), *gyaan daan* (donating knowledge or skill) and *abhay daan* (providing freedom from any fear or insecurity). In nearly all religions, *anna daan* is the most important. In Buddhism, detached and selfless generosity leads to a type of perfection called *daan paramita*. Even in Sikhism, the three duties of a true Sikh are *vand chhako* (*daan* or sharing one's earning with others), *naam japo* (recite God's name), *kirat karo* (live honestly).

The story of Akshay Patra inspires us to revisit, redefine, and reinstitutionalize these various forms of charity in the contemporary world to keep human values alive. We must awaken our social conscience and define our own Akshay Patra. This is the best way to repay our *manusya rin* (debt toward fellow human beings). We must try to make our Akshay Patra inexhaustible with not only food or material things but with everything that makes us more humane: a limitless supply of love, compassion, cooperation, forgiveness, knowledge, and much more.

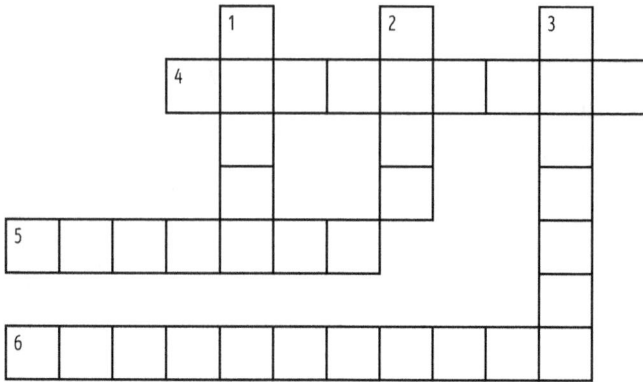

ACROSS

4 Suyodhan's common name in the Mahabharata

5 The forest where the Pandavas stayed at the start of their exile period

6 Another name for *adhik maas* (month)

DOWN

1 The god who gave Akshay Patra to Yudhisthira

2 The total number of *yugas* according to Hinduism

3 The religion that propounds the belief in *chaturvidha* of *anna daan*, abhay daan, *aushadha daan*, and *gyaan daan*

7

Subhadra haran:
Serendipity or strategy?

Marriage is the most significant *samskara* or rites of passage in Hinduism. No other *samskara* holds the power and influence of marriage. Interestingly, a general belief is that marriage is a sacred alliance that is made in heaven, whereas history offers many examples of marriages being orchestrated for important strategic reasons — economic, political, or military. Crucial strategic alliances through marriage for political and military solidarity have been seen from ancient times to the modern world. Strategic partnership through marriage was considered very strong and effective.

There are few such examples in the Mahabharata, the most significant amongst them being that of the Pandavas' marriage with Draupadi. This new relationship left the Kauravas wondering about the increase in the might and strength of the Pandavas.

After the Pandavas escaped an attempt on their
life in the wax house or *lakshagrih*, they were left
without any support and continued living in disguise
in the jungle and the outskirts of villages. After
Bhimsena slayed the demon Bakasur, the Pandavas
moved toward Ekchakranagar and stayed there for
a while. When a Brahmin informed them of King
Drupada's announcement of Draupadi's *swayamvar*,
the Pandavas, their mother Kunti, and Rishi Dhaumya
arrived in Panchala disguised as Brahmins.

The *swayamvar* stage was set. King Drupad had
declared that any warrior who could lift and string
the bow, then shoot an arrow to pierce the eye of a
golden fish suspended above a pond—while only
looking at its reflection in the water—would win
Draupadi's hand in marriage.

When the stalwarts, including Karna and
Duryodhana, failed to accomplish this difficult feat
set by King Drupad, Arjuna, disguised as a poor
Brahmin, stepped forward. He strung the mighty
bow, Kindhura, and took precise aim at the fish's
eye. The assembled Kshatriyas were stunned by the
Brahmin's remarkable act.

King Drupad then announced the marriage of
the Brahmin to Draupadi. With this alliance, the
fortunes of the Pandavas took a decisive turn, as they
now had the powerful and mighty King Drupad as
their father-in-law.

Upon learning of Draupadi's marriage to the
Pandavas, the Kauravas were filled with anxiety
and fear. They had presumed the Pandavas
to be deceased in the *lakshagriha* incident, but
now, alive and strengthened by this union, the
Pandavas posed a formidable threat. Desperately,
the Kauravas devised strategies to undermine the
alliance, considering tactics such as sowing discord
between Draupadi and her husbands or amongst
the five brothers.

Dhritarashtra agreed to welcome the Pandavas
with their new wife to Hastinapur on the suggestion
of Drona, Bhishma, Vidura, and other senior members
of the court. As a reconciliatory measure and to
honor their rightful claim to their father's kingdom,
the Pandavas were given dry, infertile, and deserted
areas of Khandavaprastha, where they could settle
down and rule. However, in some time, they turned
the barren region into a beautiful, prosperous place,
attracting scholars, Brahmins, and traders.

Once Rishi Narada visited the Pandavas and
suggested that since the five brothers had a common
wife, they should enter a privacy pact regarding
their relation with Draupadi. The pact would help
ensure that their relations with Draupadi would
not cause a rift between the brothers, weakening
them against their enemies. The pact was that
when one of the brothers was spending time with

Draupadi as a husband, the other four must not
intrude on their privacy. If anyone broke the pact,
that person would be exiled for 12 years away from
the palace. Rishi Narada narrated the example of
two asura brothers, Sunda and Upasunda, who
were inseparable and conquered all their enemies
together. However, because of a woman, Tilotma,
they fought and killed each other. Citing this story,
Rishi Narada suggested that the Pandava brothers
make and follow this pact.

However, as life poses situational dilemmas,
Arjuna was forced to break the pact as he had to
help a distressed Brahmin whose cattle were being
stolen. The desperate Brahmin accused the Pandavas
of being unable to protect their subjects. To help
the distressed Brahmin, Arjuna returned to the
palace to fetch his weapons. However, his weapons
were in the room where Yudhisthira was spending
time with Draupadi. Caught in a moral dilemma,
Arjuna decided that helping the Brahmin was more
important and broke the rule to enter the room.

When Arjuna declared that it was time for him
to start his 12-year journey, Yudhisthira tried to stop
him as he had broken the privacy pact for a good
cause. But Dhananjaya (another name for Arjuna)
insisted on undergoing the exile. As Arjuna is also
called Jishnu, the victorious one, his exile turned out
to be period of victories in his life as well as for the

Pandavas. Arjuna built a few important relations in this period, which later contributed to strengthening the Pandavas.

During exile, Arjuna married three women. The first marriage was with Naga princess Ulupi, the second was with Princess Chitrangada of Manipur, and the third and most significant marriage was with Subhadra or Bhadra, Krishna's half-sister.

At the start of the exile, Arjuna ventured to the northeastern region. One day, while Arjuna was bathing in the Ganga, the Naga princess, Ulupi, caught sight of him and was smitten by the desire to possess him. She whisked him away to the underwater kingdom of her father, King Kauravya.

Ulupi proposed marriage, but Arjuna, bound by celibacy on his pilgrimage, initially refused. Ulupi reasoned that celibacy applied only on land, and in this exile period, only with Draupadi, convincing Arjuna to marry her. Arjuna stayed with her for a few years. They had a son named Iravan. Later, Arjuna journeyed further eastward and encountered Princess Chitrangada of Manipur. He was captivated by her beauty and prowess as she was a competent warrior. Seeking her hand in marriage, Arjuna agreed to King Chitravahan's condition that Chitrangada would remain in Manipur to ensure the kingdom's lineage as Chitrangada was the king's only child. Arjuna and Chitrangada had a son named Babhruvahana in the three years he stayed with her before continuing with his travels.

Toward the second half of his exile, Arjuna visited a sacred place called Prabhasa on the west coast. Krishna heard of his arrival and came to meet Arjuna. After spending some days there with Arjuna, Krishna invited him to Dwarka. During his stay, Arjuna happened to see Subhadra, Krishna's half-sister, and captivated by her beauty, became restless. Krishna noticed Arjuna's love for Subhadra and teasingly proposed that if Arjuna wished, then he would speak to Vasudeva, his father. On hearing Krishna's words, Arjuna said that his fortunes would change if Subhadra accepted him as her husband.

After giving some thought to the subject, Krishna suggested to Arjuna that *swayamvar* was a common practice among the Kshatriyas but was not widely known among the various clans of the Yadavas, including the Andhakas, Vrishnis, Satvatas, and Abhiras, who were part of the Yadava dynasty. So, he suggested to Arjuna that among these warriors, even abduction was allowed for the purpose of marriage. However, Krishna did not mean that this kind of marriage ignored the individual choice of the woman. This is evident from a similar case in the past, when Bhishma abducted the princesses Amba, Ambika, and Ambalika for marriage with his half-brother Vichitryavira. After reaching Hastinapur,

when Amba refused the wedding as she was in love
with the King of Salva, she was respectfully sent back.
Deeply smitten by the beautiful Subhadra
and at Krishna's suggestion, Arjuna abducted
Subhadra after taking due permission through a
speedy messenger sent to Yudhisthira. The news of
Subhadra's abduction spread like wildfire in Dwarka.
The blow of a trumpet immediately called all the
able warriors to the palace. Stirred by that sound,
the Bhojas, Vrishnis, and Andhakas began to pour
in from all sides, and the chief warriors assembled in
the court. They were agitated and waited for orders
to march behind Arjuna. After some time, Baladeva
(also known as Balarama and the elder brother
of Krishna)   addressed the agitated warriors, "I
understand that you feel that this is a disrespect to us
and we must act to stop Arjuna. However, Janardana
(Krishna) is sitting quietly, seemingly unaffected
by this abduction. Let us understand what is in
his mind."

Krishna, a fine orator and best at argumentative
evaluation, spoke to the agitated warriors. He said,
"By forcibly taking Subhadra as his wife, Arjuna
has not insulted us, but rather, he has enhanced the
respect of the Yadava clan. He is an able warrior of
the Bharata race, belonging to the race of Shantanu
and born to Kunti Bhoja. Who would not wish to
be friends and family with this illustrious warrior,

the protector of *dharma*, who cannot be defeated by even Indra and Rudra but only by Mahadeva? He has chosen Subhadra as his wife. Subhadra also possesses exceptional qualities and has a good match in Arjuna. It might be that Arjuna found fault in other forms of marriage where a daughter is given away as if she is a commodity or an animal. Hence, he chose this form of marriage."

Convinced by Krishna's arguments, the warrior chiefs and Baladeva went in search of Arjuna and respectfully brought him and Subhadra back to Dwarka. In Dwarka, the elders observed Subhadra's acceptance of Arjuna, and the marriage was formally solemnized with great pomp and ceremony.

Lord Krishna, the influencer and strategist, could see the benefits of this relationship. He knew that the Pandavas should keep building strong alliances

to increase their strength. With this alliance, all the Yadava, Vrishni, and Andhaka warriors would become the Pandavas' allies, and the relation based on this marriage would be strong and lifelong. Krishna's understanding of the future of the Kauravas and Pandavas' relationship would have led him not to miss this golden opportunity to get the Pandavas close to the Yadavas and also to arrange a compatible alliance for his sister, Subhadra. Lord Krishna helped the Pandavas go from strength to strength in this one act.

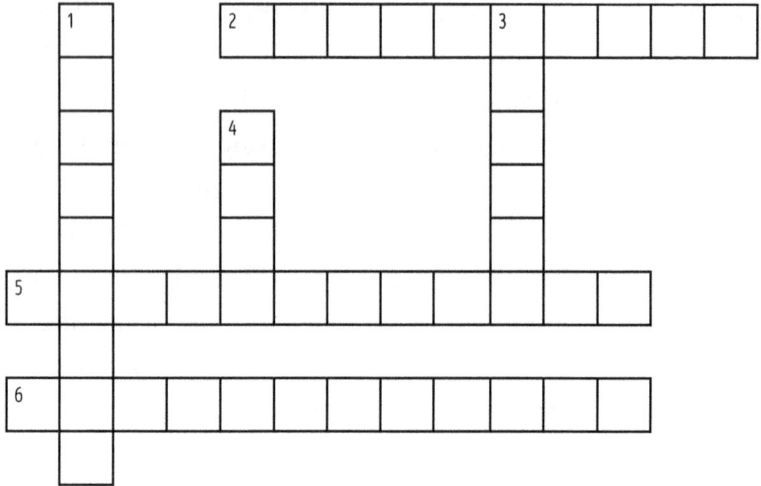

ACROSS

2 Musician at Indra's palace who taught Arjuna the music of the celestials

5 The king of Manipur and father of Princess Chitrangada—one of Arjuna's wives

6 The name given to the Pandavas' capital at Khandavaprastha

DOWN

1 Duryodhana's trusted aide, who was given the task of making the lakshagriha to kill the Pandavas in the fire

3 The Pandava brother who was ambidextrous

4 The total number of Arjuna's wives, including Draupadi

8

Amba reborn as Shikhandi:
Gender fluidity for a purpose

In Hindu philosophy, *nirguna* Brahman is the ultimate truth, formless and beyond gender distinctions. Ascribing qualities to Brahman limits its infinite nature. The method of *neti-neti* or "not this, not this" negates all descriptions of Brahman, including gender, illustrating that characteristics restrict Brahman's boundless essence. This method of defining Brahman by *neti-neti*, observed in the Brihadaranyaka Upanishad and extensively used in Advaita Vedanta, underscores the fluidity of all types of forms including gender. While *saguna* Brahman, or personal gods, possess distinct attributes, they maintain fluidity in gender and form. Examples include Lord Vishnu as Mohini, Lord Shiva as Ardhanarishwar, and Lord Krishna's diverse manifestations emphasizing feminine traits. Even celestial entities like Budha (the lord of planet Mercury) are considered to be neuter in gender, and revered deities like Gopeshwar Mahadev exhibit gender-fluid roles, reflecting the nuanced understanding of self and identity in Hinduism.

In Hinduism, the interconnected and overlapping themes of life's purpose, rebirth, and karmic conse-quences from past lives are intricately woven. The story of Shikhandi and Bhishma, apart from having all of the themes of purpose, rebirth, and the karmic balance sheet, has an added layer of complexity with gender fluidity interestingly woven into these themes.

Bhishma (Devavrata) and Shikhandi are important and celebrated characters in the Mahabharata. Bhishma Pitamah, the great-grandfather of the Pandavas and Kauravas, was seen as an upholder of *dharma*. He was known for the difficult vow or oath he had taken for the happiness of his father, King Shantanu, who wanted to marry Satyavati. Bhishma took a vow to remain celibate his entire life and act as a guardian to his half-siblings born to Shantanu and Satyavati. It was a difficult promise, but he lived up to it. From this terrible vow of Bhishma, the standard term of *Bhishma pratigya* became famous for referring to any undoable or challenging oath. Following this rigid vow, King Shantanu blessed Devavrata or Bhishma with the boon of *icchha mrityu* or the ability to choose the time of death.

Shikhandi was born with no apparent gender

(gender fluid) to King Drupada. Shikhandi, who was Princess Amba in a previous life, was responsible for killing Bhishma Pitamah in the Kurukshetra war. Princess Amba and Bhishma Pitamah's lives were intertwined by a purpose and karmic consequences, which were achieved through Amba's rebirth as Shikhandi.

Going a little back in the story, Bhishma abducted the three daughters of the king of Kashipur — Amba, Ambika, and Ambalika — from their *swayamvar* ceremony to get them married to his half-brother, Vichitravirya — Satyavati and Shantanu's son. If, on the one hand, Bhishma is celebrated for his *pratigya*, on the other hand, he is also known for the wrong he committed by abducting the three sisters against their wishes. In ensuring the welfare of his half-brother, he committed the crime of sacrificing the three princesses' freedom of choice.

When Bhishma entered the *swayamvar* ceremony of the three sisters, he announced his intention and was open to fighting with anyone who challenged him. King Salva, who was in love with the eldest princess, Amba, tried to counter Bhishma but was defeated. Bhishma reached Hastinapur with the three princesses, and Satyavati started preparing for the marriage. However, just before the ceremony, Amba, the eldest princess, conveyed her feelings to the gathering of sages and scholars, saying that she was committed to Salva and could not marry Vichitravirya.

Amba was sent back to King Salva, but he did not accept her because she had been abducted, and Salva had lost the fight with Bhishma. Dejected, she proceeded into the deep jungle. According to another version of the story, after being rejected by Salva, she approached Bhishma to marry her as he was responsible for her plight. But because of his vow of celibacy, Bhishma could not accept the proposal.

Disheartened, Amba began a deep penance in the jungle to avenge her loss. According to one version of the story, moved by her deep penance, Lord Shiva blessed her to be born as a man and a great warrior who would remember her purpose against Bhishma and kill him. According to another version, Lord Karthikeya gifted Amba a garland of ever-fresh flowers and said that whoever wore that garland could defeat anyone, including Bhishma. However, being a woman, she could not bring Bhishma to fight her. She requested many kings, including Drupada, who refused to pick a war with Bhishma. Frustrated, Amba left the garland at Drupada's palace gate, went into the deep jungle, and ended her life.

In her next life, she was born to Drupada as Shikhandi. King Drupada, who was childless, was undergoing a deep penance for a child, and Lord Shiva granted him his wish. Shikhandi, Draupadi, and Drishtadyumna were born to Drupada, of whom Shikhandi was Amba reborn.

Since birth, Shikhandi's gender was unclear or somewhat fluid, as he displayed both feminine and masculine characteristics. Despite having a fluid gender, he was well accepted in Drupada's palace and was trained to be a great warrior.

After the Pandavas married the Panchal princess, Draupadi, King Drupada and the entire kingdom of Panchal became the Pandavas' allies. Aware of the warrior skills of Draupadi's brother, Shikhandi, the Pandavas made him the commander of one of the seven *akshauhinis* of their army during the Kurukshetra war. The Pandavas did not discriminate against him because of his androgynous status. In the Kurukshetra war, he made a significant contribution by being the cause of Bhishma Pitamah's death, which was essential for the Pandavas' side, and at the same time, fulfilled the purpose of his previous birth as Amba.

The gender fluidity of Shikhandi was to grant him the flexibility to achieve his objective.

On the battlefield, Bhishma lowered his bow when Shikhandi faced him. According to some versions, Bhishma recognised Amba reborn as Shikhandi and thus lowered his arm. According to some, Shikhandi exhibited a feminine form at that moment. Bhishma, not wanting to attack a woman, dropped his bow, and at that moment, Arjuna, ready behind Shikhandi, shot Bhishma.

The story of Shikhandi and Bhishma Pitamah offers profound insights into Hindu philosophy, emphasizing the fluidity of gender and the inter-connected themes of *karma*, rebirth and life's purpose. Both Bhishma and Shikhandi were driven by the sense of duty and purpose. Bhishma had to fulfill his vow of celibacy and his commitment to safeguard the lineage of his half-brothers, while

Shikhandi's quest was the fulfillment of his past life's purpose. Despite Shikhandi's unconventional gender identity, he is accepted and respected within the community, which emphasizes the importance of an inclusive society. The story beautifully reveals the moral complexities and ethical dilemmas faced in life by virtuous persons. Bhishma's conflicting role as an upholder of *dharma* and his involvement in the abduction of the three princesses exposes us to the idea that individuals may be both virtuous and flawed, and their actions can have far-reaching consequences. The intertwined destinies of Bhishma and Shikhandi highlight the intricate relation of *karma* and rebirth in Hindu belief and how past actions and relationships determine interactions in subsequent lives, strongly demonstrating the concept of *karma phal* (the fruits of our actions).

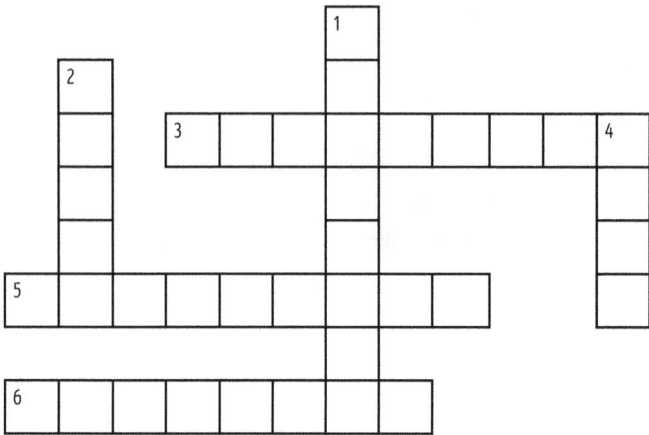

ACROSS

3 Bhishma Pitamah's childhood name

5 Vichitravirya's mother

6 The commander-in-chief of the Panchala army in King Drupada's reign; popularly known as Chitraratha in the Mahabharata

DOWN

1 Shikhandi's sister

2 The king who tried to counter Bhishma's attempt to kidnap the three sisters—Amba, Ambika, and Ambalika—from their *swayamvar*

4 One of the three princesses abducted by Bhishma for marriage to his half-brother, Vichitravirya

9

Ahankara:
Guard it tight to get it right!

The realms of psychology, philosophy, religion, and science have long been captivated by the intricacies of the mind. *Antahkaran*, the Sanskrit word, encompasses the totality of the mind and its functions and is widely adopted by all schools of Indian philosophy. Renowned poet Kalidas asserts that *antahkaran* provides absolute clarity during conflict of thought, serving as a final guide in moral dilemmas.

The significance of *antahkaran* is profound, as evidenced by extensive discussions across various schools of Indian philosophy, all acknowledging and recognizing its formidable power. According to Vedanta philosophy, *antahkaran* consists of *ahamkara*, *buddhi*, *manas*, and *chitta*. *Ahamkara* is the most consequential amongst these as one needs to guard against it. Unguarded or unchecked *ahamkara* has tremendous power to uproot even the mightiest person. Ravana, a scholar and powerful Shiva *bhakta*, fell prey to his own *ahamkara*. Ravana's *ahamkara* killed him; Lord Rama was an instrument to accomplish the task. Duryodhana, the eldest Kuru prince, could have enjoyed his life, surrounded by learned people, scholars, and sages. However, his *ahamkara* led him to believe that he was the most superior and deserved to be the crown prince. It was Duryodhana's untamed *ahamkara* that killed him. There are several similar stories of Lord Indra falling prey to his own fatal *ahamkara*.

The "I Doer," *ahamkara*, or the one that creates a sense of possessiveness and ego, made Indra believe that he was the supreme being in the entire universe. Once, his untamed ego made him relinquish his throne as the king of the devas, and another time, he was punished to be reborn as a human being, undergoing the trials and tribulations of human life as a repentance.

These two significant stories of Lord Indra's unchecked *ahamkara* show the heavy price we pay for unbridled desires coupled with *ahamkara*.

The first story is that of the war between Lord Indra and the demon Vritta. Lord Indra faced a grave threat from Vritta, who had controlled the entire world's water, causing widespread unrest. Seeking help, the devas approached Lord Indra who in turn went to Lord Vishnu. Lord Vishnu advised them to

create a special weapon (*vajrayuddha*) from the bones
of Sage Dadhichi (who happily agreed to sacrifice
himself for the larger cause) to defeat Vritta. After
a long war, Indra emerged victorious with the help
of *vajrayuddha* and Lord Vishnu, who helped him
escape from Vritta's stomach when Indra along with
his vehicle, Airawat, was swallowed by Vritta.

After the victory, Indra was welcomed like a hero
by the devas. However, over time, Indra forgot the
contributions of Sage Dadhichi and Lord Vishnu
in his victory and falsely thought himself to be
unparalleled and invincible. He commissioned the
the divine architect, Vishwakarma, to construct a
magnificent palace that would match Indra's new
stature. However, his insatiable desire for grandeur
led to frustration and exhaustion for the divine
architect. Vishwakarma sought the intervention
of Lord Brahma, Lord Shiva, and Lord Vishnu,
explaining the perpetual cycle of Indra's demands.

Lord Vishnu and Lord Shiva assured Vishwakarma that they would address the issue. The next
day, as Indra admired his palace, a young boy
approached him. Indra proudly asked the boy if he
had ever seen a palace more marvelous than this one.
The boy said that none of the earlier Indras had such
a magnificent palace. Surprised, Lord Indra asked
him if there were any other Indras before him.

The boy, Lord Shiva in disguise, revealed the

cyclical nature of Indra's existence. Each time Lord
Brahma created a new universe, a new Indra was
appointed, and the cycle continued.

The boy pointed to a line of ants on the ground
representing previous Indras who had fallen from
grace due to their unchecked ego. As Indra was
struggling with this revelation, an old man with
a peculiar circular pattern of chest hair appeared.
On being asked why most of his hair had fallen in
a peculiar pattern, he explained that every time an
Indra fell from his position, a hair fell. Indra realized
the gravity of his unchecked ego and willingly
relinquished his throne, retreating to a secluded place
to practice austerity and do penance for his sins.

The second story, found in the Vaivahika Parva
of the Mahabharata, has an equally profound lesson

for us. Once, Lord Indra was sitting beside River Bhagirathi and noticed a golden lotus being carried along the river's current. Desirous of seeing where the golden lotus had come from, he walked toward the source of the river. At one point, he noticed a beautiful woman beside the river. She was weeping, and as her tears fell, they turned into golden lotus flowers. Indra asked her why she was crying. She replied that he must come along with her and see for himself.

As Lord Indra followed her, the lady took him near a beautiful stream, where a young man was engaged in a game of dice with a woman. The man did not bother to acknowledge the presence of Lord Indra and continued playing his game.

Lord Indra addressed the young man and said, "Hey, young man, you must know that this world is under my control." However, the young man remained engrossed in his game. Furious, Lord Indra said, "I am the lord of this universe." The young man, who was none other than Lord Shiva, glanced at Lord Indra, which almost paralyzed him. He told Indra, "You will have to pay for this excessive ego and pride so that you dare not behave in this way ever."

Lord Shiva asked Indra to remove a huge stone at the mouth of the cave nearby and go inside. Inside the cave, there were four others who looked like Indra.

Lord Shiva said that once, even these Indras had the power and splendor of the Sun, but because of their uncontrolled ego, they were punished to restrain themselves in the cave. Seeing their plight, Indra was shaken. With folded hands, he prayed to Lord Shiva to forgive him. Rejecting his appeal, Lord Shiva said that any person with uncontrolled *ahamkara* would not receive His grace.

Lord Shiva further addressed the four Indras and said they would take birth as human beings. After facing the difficulties, trials, and tribulations of human life and adhering to *dharma* in the most challenging situations, they would achieve the merits of their *karma* and regain their place among the divine.

However, the current Indra requested Lord Shiva that he should be allowed to create a fifth person from a part of his own body, who would be reborn as a human along with the other four Indras.

Lord Shiva then took them to Lord Narayana (Vishnu) and consulted him about Indra's plea. Lord Narayana approved of Lord Shiva's decision and added to the plan by sending two men created from parts of his own body to the earth along with the five Indras. The two men born on earth were Krishna and Baladeva.

The Pandavas were the five Indras (four past and one current Indra) reborn as humans, and celestial

Shree reincarnated as Draupadi to be the common wife to the Indras.

Thus, the Pandavas, the Indras born in human form, faced the vagaries of life, still maintained their steadfastness to *dharma*, and ultimately regained their position as celestial beings. Despite the atrocities committed by their cousins and their uncle, Dhritarashtra who was also their guardian, the Pandavas maintained their composure and did not resort to unethical means.

This story beautifully weaves the despair of Lord Indra and the hope that Lord Shiva offered to him to regain his celestial position after undergoing the life of a human being. The story is a reminder that if even Lord Indra had to repent for his untamed *ahamkara*, we, as mortal humans, would have no respite from the consequences of having an uncontrolled ego. However, this story gives us the hope of a chance to rectify our mistakes.

Lord Shiva's reply to Indra that "No one who has this kind of ego receives my grace" is a message to practice humility. Lord Shiva shows an example of participative leadership by approaching Lord Narayana for his input. Lord Narayana gives his valuable input to the scheme like an able leader. A true leader molds his *ahamkara* to make it their strength rather than their weakness.

Since *ahamkara* is one of the inner functions of

the *antahkaran* and an essential part of the human mind, no one is free from it. The power of *ahamkara*, if harnessed properly, becomes excellent willpower, the strength of determination or self-power. If *ahamkara* goes unharnessed, it can uproot even the most powerful.

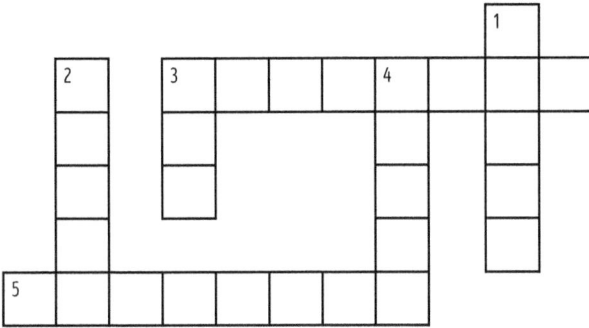

ACROSS

3 The great sage who contributed his bones to make the weapon, vajrayuddha, to defeat the demon Vritta

5 Indra's elephant

DOWN

1 Ravana was the devout follower of this god

2 The name of the festival celebrated in Telangana, Andhra Pradesh, Tamil Nadu, and Karnataka to worship Lord Indra, the god of rains and clouds, to bring good rain, harvest, and prosperity

3 In Varanasi, this Deepavali is celebrated on Kartik Purnima to mark the killing of the demon Tripurasur by Lord Shiva

4 A prominent Rigvedic god

10

Nala and Damayanti:
The story which redeemed Yudhisthira

Stories are powerful. They can change our mood, beliefs, and perspectives. Storytelling has the power to engage, influence, teach, and inspire listeners. Tell a story to a person who has lost hope and is in despair. Tell a story when a person is in self-doubt since skilful storytelling is therapeutic. This science of storytelling is not new, but wise mentors and teachers have endorsed it as an art since antiquity.

In the Varna Parva of the Mahabharata, Sage Vrihadaswa tells a story to raise Yudhisthira's self-confidence, because he was facing severe self-doubt and seemed to forget his duty. The sage understands the criticality of the situation and acts immediately by narrating to him the story of Nala and Damayanti. Had Rishi Vrihadaswa not done this, then Yudhisthira would probably have gone into deeper self-doubt, losing his confidence and future purpose. After

Yudhisthira had lost everything in the game of dice and the Pandavas were forced into forest exile, Sage Vrihadaswa visited Yudhisthira. The sage observed the self-accusatory state of mind and the feeling of deep self-doubt, and decided to tell Yudhisthira the story of Nala and Damayanti.

Damayanti, the princess of the Vidarbha kingdom, was known for her unmatched beauty and intelligence. Stories of her beauty were widespread among gods, demons, and humans. Many gods had heard about her qualities, and many among them suitors for Damayanti. There was an equally extensive list of earthly kings who wanted to marry her.

At the same time, there lived King Nala of the Nishad kingdom. Nala was a good-looking and successful ruler, and his kingdom prospered under him. He was an able administrator, well versed in the Vedas, a skilled charioteer, and a cook par excellence. One day, Nala found a swan with golden wings in the garden of his inner quarters and caught it. The swan, desirous of being freed, made an offer to King Nala. The swan said that if Nala freed it, it would fly to Damayanti and speak to her about the illustrious Nala and how Nala was the best suitor for her amongst all men, gods, gandharvas, and demons. The swan told Nala about the beautiful Damayanti, whom even the gods wished to marry, but stated that Nala would be the right husband for her.

Nala set the swan free, and as promised, the swan described the valor and beauty of Nala to Damayanti. On hearing Nala's praises, Damayanti wanted to meet and marry him. In due course, King Bhima, Damayanti's father, announced her *swayamvar*, causing excitement among humans, celestials, demons, and gandharvas, who desired to win Damayanti.

Nala, too, left for the kingdom of Vidarbha to participate in the *swayamvar*. On the way, he met the guardian of the universe, Indra, and other gods — Agni, Varuna, and Yama. All the four gods requested him to be their messenger to Damayanti and tell her that the celestials were desirous of obtaining her and would be participating in the *swayamvar*. Since Nala wanted Damayanti for himself, he pleaded to the gods that he would not be the right choice to be the messenger. However, the gods still asked him to go ahead and be their messenger. Damayanti, upon knowing the feelings of the gods, was shaken, but her desire to choose Nala did not change. It strengthened instead when she saw him, in reality, standing in front of her as the messenger of the celestials. Nala conveyed Damayanti's message to the gods that she was only interested in choosing Nala as her husband.

On the day of the *swayamvar*, all four gods assumed the look of Nala and sat along with him. Damayanti was confused to see five Nalas, and in extreme anxiety, she prayed to those gods that since she desired only Nala as her husband, they must guide and bless her to choose the right Nala. The gods, moved by her love for Nala, blessed her to identify the original Nala.

However, her wedding to Nala did not go down well with one of the demons, Kali, who vowed to take revenge. He stayed with Nala like a shadow and waited for 12 years to find a weakness in Nala and overpowered him. After possessing Nala, Kali guided him to play the game of dice with his brother, Pushkara. Nala lost everything in the game. He and his wife were deserted and took refuge in a forest. Still possessed by Kali, Nala abandoned his wife, Damayanti, in the woods. After wandering for some days, Damayanti took refuge in the court of King Chedi.

Meanwhile, Nala moved into the deep jungle, where a serpent, Naga, bit him. The bite turned out to be a blessing in disguise, for it changed him into a dwarf with short arms. Nala assumed a new name, Vahuka, for this disguise. However, Naga blessed Nala with a cloth that he could wear to get his original looks back whenever he wished to. In disguise as Vahuka, Nala found refuge with the King of Ayodhya, Rituparna, who was a skilled dice player.

Soon, Damyanti's father, King Bhima, found her and took her to his palace. Damayanti could not forget Nala and was keen on finding him. She sent Brahmins and spies to discover Nala's whereabouts. Through one of the Brahmins, she learned about someone in King Rituparna's kingdom who was a great charioteer and cook. She was sure that it could not be a coincidence that someone had both the qualities peculiar to Nala.

Damayanti resolved to bring back her husband and planned a trick. She announced her *swayamvar* again and ensured that King Rituparna got the message. She sent the message that after the dawn of the sun the next day, King Bhima would organize Damayanti's *swayamvar*. King Rituparna, having heard of the beautiful and intelligent Damayanti, decided to participate in the *swayamvar*. He got his most skilled charioteer, Vahuka, to ride him to

King Bhima's palace as there was not enough time for the *swayamvar*. Vahuka (Nala) drove Rituparna to the kingdom of Vidharba. Damayanti, alert to all the guests coming to the kingdom for the *swayamvar*, identified the hoofbeats of Nala's horse when he drove in as King Rituparna's charioteer. The confirmation of Damayanti's suspicion came from the message that King Rituparna had declined King Bhima's hospitality, as he would prefer eating the food prepared by his skilled cook, Vahuka. Now sure of his identity, Damayanti confronted Nala. On seeing Damayanti in front of him, Nala could not control himself and assumed his original look.

King Rituparna understood the situation, empathized with Nala and Damayanti, and appreciated their deep love for each other. He promised to help them get their kingdom back. Nala stayed with Rituparna for some more time and learned the art of dice from the skilled king. Once he was confident about his dice skills, Nala challenged Pushkara to play the game again. Pushkara, not fully satisfied with his previous win, since he could not win Damayanti then, accepted Nala's offer. However, without Kali's support, Pushkara lost the game. Nala got his kingdom back, and he and Damayanti lived happily ever after.

The story was wisely put forth by Sage Vrihadaswa when he found Yudhisthira at a very critical juncture in his life. Vrihadaswa, a wise mentor, knew the art of counseling through storytelling. Through relevant stories, people in situations of crisis and hopelessness get the feeling of not being alone or not being the only ones to face difficulties. The story sends a powerful message to a defeated mind that there are ways out of the complex and challenging situation, and people have fought more difficult situations than theirs in the past.

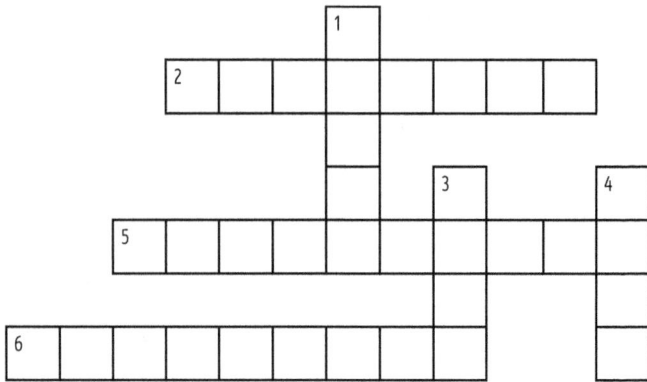

ACROSS

2 The total number of Parvas in the Mahabharata

5 The sage who narrated the story of Nala and Damayanti to Yudhisthira

6 After losing the game of dice, Nala, in disguise, became a charioteer to this king

DOWN

1 Damayanti's father

3 Damayanti's husband, known for his great cooking skills

4 The demon who convinced Nala to play a game of dice with his brother, Pushkara, in which Nala lost everything he had

11

Chandra:
The retainer of our mind loses his heart

The exhilarating Chandra or Somadeva (the moon god) is the ruler of people's minds. There are various mantras for people to chant and invoke the blessings of Lord Chandra for mental peace and prosperity. He is also one of the sacred Navagrahas (the nine planets that are believed to influence human life on the Earth). In contrast to this position of Lord Chandra, there is an intriguing story where Chandra, the regulator of our mind, loses his heart to Devi Tara, the wife of Lord Brahaspati (Jupiter).

Jupiter, or Guru, (Brahaspati), the chief priest of the gods, was rational and practical. His beautiful wife, Tara, on the other hand, was a passionate woman desirous of intense love. Once, Brahaspati had to go to Chandra's house to perform a *yagna*. Since the wife has a significant position in ancient traditions—symbolizing the importance of women and the *grihastha ashram* (the stage of being a married person) — the rituals could not be completed without the presence of the wife. So, Tara accompanied Brahaspati. The attractive and passionate Chandra met the captivating and lovelorn Tara. Both were attracted to each other and fell in love.

As love knows no boundaries, Tara moved to stay with Chandra. However, it was awkward because Tara was the wife of the guru of the gods and even Chandra's guru.

This act of Tara and Chandra caused huge embarrassment to Brahaspati, who requested Chandra to send Tara back. Brahaspati appealed to the rationale of *dharma*: Tara was a married woman, and she was the wife of Chandra's guru. Chandra had an equally strong appeal to make. He felt that Brahaspati was committing *adharma* by keeping Tara with him because there was no love between them. Unity without true intimacy and mutual feeling is not *dharma* and is not considered a virtuous partnership. The relationship also needs to be under the tenets of *dharma*. This aspect of the story conveys the beauty of the Hindu religion — that it is ever-evolving and each individual is free to find their own truth and be guided by their own belief. There are no rigid dictums that guide our lives.

Lord Indra was bound to interfere between the two parties, for he feared that Brahaspati might

refuse to continue as the guru of the devas. Indra was highly dependent on Brahaspati for the rituals to maintain his position. Tension mounted on both sides. It was the clash of ego and love, both equally strong and aptly taking refuge under *dharma*. So, apprehending a war, Indra felt it right to interfere.

Indra compelled Tara to return to Brahaspati, paving the way for the superiority of the *dharma* of a wife to the *dharma* of a lover. However, Tara was carrying a child at the time. Brahaspati asked her who the father was, but Tara refused to reply. Some versions of the story say that it was Lord Brahma in whom Tara confided, whereas others say that when Tara declined to answer Brahaspati's question, the unborn child spoke from Tara's womb and told her that a child had the right to know who his father was.

To this, Devi Tara replied that Lord Chandra was the father of the child. Full of rage, Brahaspati cursed the unborn child to be born in the neuter gender. Another version says that after Tara gave birth, Lord Chandra took the child away, putting it under the care of his wife, Rohini.

Born out of the union of Chandra (mind) and Tara (youth and beauty), Budha or Mercury is youthful and represents the intellect and the mind, differentiating good from evil. While Chandra is an innocent, calm mind, Budha is a discerning mind.

In the tangled cosmic drama, the tale of Chandra, Tara, and Brahaspati unfolds with layers of love, duty, and cosmic balance. The clash between ego and love, examined within the principles of *dharma*, illuminates the fluidity and evolution inherent in Hindu beliefs. In the background of the celestial conflict, Lord Indra's effort to precariously balance the supremacy of the *dharma* of a wife over that of a lover and Tara's return to Brahaspati, despite the love she shared with Chandra, symbolizes the prioritization of duty and societal norms. Budha's birth out of Tara and Chandra's love symbolizes that intellect is born from a calm mind. This celestial saga echoes the ever-changing nature of Hindu philosophy, where individuals navigate their own truths, guided by belief rather than rigid dictums.

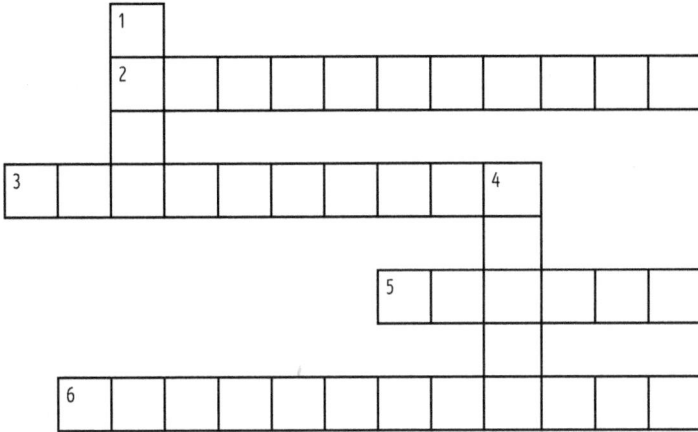

ACROSS

2 The total number of wives Chandra is believed to have

3 The chief priest of the gods

5 Devi Tara and Lord Chandra's love-child

6 The guru or priest of the demons

DOWN

1 Chandra's father and a famous sage

4 The god who took steps to resolve the conflict between Chandra and Brahaspati

12

Lopamudra and Agastya:
Exploring the relationship

A meaningful relationship is at the core of human social life. Of the various types of relationships, the need to develop a fulfilling romantic relationship is the most profound. A relationship that helps an individual achieve their purpose in life harmoniously under the guidance of *dharma* is the most pious. As relationship experts and counselors either look for a quick-fix formula or a well-researched key to this harmonious relationship, here is a story from the Rigveda which gives an insight into ancient alliances and their purpose.

Welcome to the enlightened world of Lopamudra and Agastya, where the creator depends on his creation to realize his goals. Neither claims ultimate superiority; instead, they share a synergetic relation.

Here, the producer becomes a *yachak* (seeker) to his creation. Though the creation owes its existence to the creator, it simultaneously places conditions that the creator is bound to fulfill.

Lopamudra, the Brahmavadini (the knower of supreme knowledge), the perfect beauty, gives purpose to her creator. In this world, the creator does not dominate his creation but seeks her favors for worldly obligations.

Two prominent sources that describe Lopamudra's life are the Rigveda and the Mahabharata. She is also known by the names of Kaushitaki or Varaprada. According to the Rigveda, Lopamudra and Agastya are *mantra drashta* (seers) credited with creating mantras. Her Rigvedic mantras dedicated to Rati (goddess of love) symbolize her freedom to choose and describe an enabler who explores her sexuality like any other material desire and openly discusses it. The hymns dedicated to her in the

Rigveda indicate the significance of a householder's life and the incompleteness of an ascetic practice that ignores domestic duties. She mentors and guides Rishi Agastya to balance his life as an ascetic with his life as a householder since both obligations are supreme and ignoring a householder's duties is a sin. She helps Agastya attain immortality by balancing both responsibilities. Lopamudra is the equilibrium in Agastya's life as she guides him to balance his ascetic and householder duties. She is an essential element in Agastya's journey to fulfill his worldly obligations, which is a prerequisite for liberation. In the Rigvedic context, she is a scholar who fulfills, demands, and enables.

According to another source, Lopamudra was created by Rishi Agastya as his ancestors demanded that he marry and beget a son to help them gain liberation. Agastya then started creating a woman of rare beauty. Taking inspiration from nature, he gave her the eyes of a doe, the grace of a panther, the slenderness of palm trees, the fragrance of the *champak* flower, and the softness of the feathers on a swan's neck. The name Lopamudra signifies the loss (*lopa*) that the animals and plants suffered by giving their distinctive features (*mudra*) when Agastya created her. Therefore, the making of Lopamudra is metaphoric of the beauty in the universe and our dependence on it to bring out perfection in our lives. When the most beautiful and intelligent human being was to be created, the inspiration and contribution came from other living beings that coexist on this planet.

After Agastya had created Lopamudra, he gifted her to the king of Vidarbha, who was undergoing extreme penance in his desire for a child. The king happily accepted Lopamudra. Once Lopamudra was of marriageable age, Rishi Agastya approached the king and asked for Lopamudra's hand in marriage. The king was anguished at the proposal of marrying his princess to a poor forest dweller double her age, but he was equally scared at the prospect of denying the request of a great sage. However, Lopamudra requested her father to marry her to Agastya.

When Agastya wanted to beget a child with her, she put a condition of wanting royal comfort before their procreation. This precondition of Lopamudra and Agastya's fulfillment of the condition symbolizes the respect and importance of women and their consent in domestic life. Considering that it was a husband's duty to honor the wife's words and fulfill her desires, Agastya asked the three rich kings, Srutarvan, Vradhnaswa, and Trasadasyu, for help. The three kings showed him their kingdoms' balance sheets and expressed their helplessness as they could not spare anything. However, they advised Rishi Agastya to approach the king of the asuras and seek wealth from him. Rishi met Illwala, the king of the asuras, and deceived him by killing his brother, Vatapi. Illwala then surrendered and gave all his riches to Rishi Agastya.

The creation of Lopamudra and the fulfillment of Agastya's obligations point to the limitations of our existence, interdependency, and the necessity of coexistence.

Agastya creates a woman—the most beautiful and intelligent woman—using contributions from the best of other living beings. This indicates our dependency on the natural environment despite being the most evolved species on the globe. It directs us to appreciate the beauty of others.

No one in this world is self-sufficient. Even the most scholarly person, the *mantra drashta* (Agastya), who had powers to create the most beautiful human being, depended on Lopamudra (his creation) to liberate his ancestors. He could bless a childless king with a child, but he could not accomplish his purpose independently.

The story also eulogizes the duties of a person in *grihastha ashram*—the most powerful of sages went seeking for riches to fulfill his wife's desire for them.

The approach of Agastya to ask for riches from the biggest of kings, Srutarvan, exposes us to the principles the kings followed at that time. Srutarvan shared his revenues and expenses with Agastya, who

understood that there was nothing extra for the king
to give away. The king utilized the entire income
for the welfare of his subjects. Agastya observed a
similar situation with the other two kings.

Apart from being one of the famous Brahmavadinis
who strove for the highest philosophical knowledge,
Lopamudra contributed to matriarchal theology. She
has to her credit the composition of the Nadi Pancha
Dasi mantra of the Shakta tradition (Shakta tradition
within Hinduism is a goddess-centric institution
where Shakti, feminine energy, is the main deity).
She is a representative of feminine divine power,
which is a vital characteristic of the Hindu religion.

This ancient story unearths timeless lessons
that resonate in the essence of meaningful
relationships—with fellow humans, with ecology,
with our duties. Lopamudra, the Brahmavadini,
emerges as a symbol of purpose and freedom, and
as an enabler, navigating the realms of ascetic and
householder duties. Her union with Agastya not
only signifies the interdependence of creation but
also highlights the beauty found in the collaborative
contributions of various organisms, emphasizing
our connection to the environment. The conditions
set by Lopamudra and Agastya's pursuit of wealth
underscore the respect and importance of women's
acceptance in domestic life, as well as the profound
duties of individuals in *grihastha ashram*. This ancient

saga, while celebrating the highest philosophical knowledge and feminine divine power, leaves us with a poignant reminder — that no one in this world is truly self-sufficient, and our existence thrives on interdependency, coexistence, and the appreciation of the beauty found beyond ourselves.

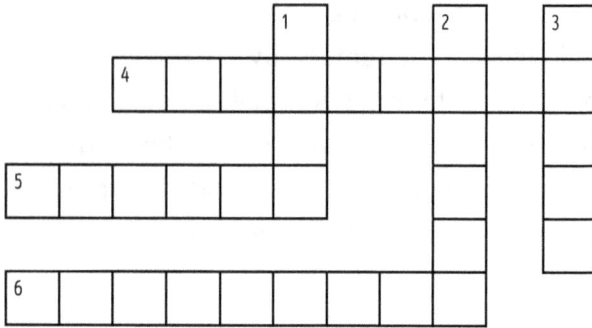

ACROSS

4 Another name for Lopamudra
5 Atapi's demon brother, who was digested by Rishi Agastya
6 The art of illusion exclusively known to the gandharvas, which was imparted to Arjuna after he defeated a Gandharva

DOWN

1 Goddess of love
2 The river in South India associated with Lopamudra
3 The Upanishad that contains the famous dialogue between Nachiketa and Yamaraj

13

Prajapati's eternal teaching:
Da... Da... Da..

The Brihadaranyaka Upanishad, the store house of wisdom and knowledge, has eternal teachings that transcend time, era, and region. Among various wise teachings put forth in the Brihadaranyaka Upanishad through intriguing stories and narratives, the story of the creator, Prajapati, and his three descendants—gods (devas), humans (manushya), and demons (asuras)—is a lesson well crafted for modern times. The story enforces the life wisdom that the meaning of words and situations depends on our perception, understanding, past experiences, and environment. The story exposes us to the interplay of the predominant *gunas*—*sattva, rajas,* and *tamas*— in guiding our actions and creating different mental dispositions that lead to diverse interpretations of the same situation, words, and experiences.

The story from the Brihadaranyaka Upanishad is

about the three descendants of the creator, Prajapati
(Brahma) — devas, manushya, and asuras, who
practiced *brahmacharya* (celibacy) under Prajapati's
guidance. On completion of their years of study,
the three descendants approached Prajapati and
requested him for the final teaching or *upadesha* to
practice in their lives.

First, the gods approached and requested him
for his final teaching. Prajapati uttered "द (Da)" and
asked the gods if they understood. The gods said they
did, elaborating that the word meant *damayata* or self-
control. Prajapati agreed that they had understood it
correctly and blessed them.

The humans approached him next, and Prajapati
said "द (Da)" again. He asked the humans if they
understood their final teaching. The humans said

they understood, and it meant *daata* or doing
charity. Prajapati accepted their understanding and
blessed them.

Finally, the demons also requested for their
teaching. Prajapati again repeated "द (Da)" and
asked the demons if they understood the meaning.
The demons said that they understood the *upadesh*
(teaching), and "द (Da)" according to them, was
dayadhvam or being compassionate. Prajapati agreed
that the demons had understood their teaching and
blessed them too.

This story unveils a deep philosophical thought.
It shows that the meaning of any word or situation
depends on our perception, understanding, past
experiences, and the environment. It also shows
how the predominant *guna* (*sattva*, *rajas*, or *tamas*)
guides our actions and mental disposition, leading
to varied perceptions.

The gods are blessed with unlimited pleasures
of all kinds in devaloka. They have plenty of
everything, and they don't need to sweat and toil
to earn their living. They are used to unilimited
pleasure and endless comfort, and they do not age
either. Given this easy, pleasure-filled existence, the
devas needed to practice self-control so that divinity
can predominate and continue.

Humans have a tendency to acquire and hoard.
Even if we have plenty, the greed does not end, and

we do not want to give away our acquisitions. We want more of everything, be it assets, money, or comfort. So, to retain our humaneness, we need to practice charity. We should not keep more than we need. Apart from giving away material possessions, charity could also be in the form of cooperation, knowledge, forgiveness, love, care, and much more. In a broader context, charity also implies not possessing what we do not need or what does not belong to us.

Demons have substantial physical strength, and they are cruel by nature. They are violent and destructive and cannot distinguish between good and evil easily. So, they need to practice compassion to keep their negativity in control.

As individuals, we struggle with all three of these negative traits — the general inclination of the mind toward objects of pleasure, the tendency of the mind to seize or possess material objects beyond our capacity to utilize them, and the tendency of the mind to seek pleasure in the grief of others. These are the three weakness of gods, humans, and demons respectively that they needed to control. But as individuals, we all have all three aspects — divinity, humaneness, and demonic traits — in us. To maintain the divine element, we need to practice self-control; to preserve our humaneness, we need to practice charity; and finally, to control the demonic aspect, we need to practice compassion or mercy. *Damyata* (self-control), *daan* (charity), and *dayadhvam* (compassion) are the three magical and spiritual teachings to be practiced for a fuller and richer life. To keep progressing toward the final goal of *moksha* or liberation, we need to practice all three.

Prajapati Brahma accepted the meaning as understood by each of his descendants and did not give any fixed meaning to his teaching. It was left open to interpretation, and the teacher wholeheartedly agreed with each interpretation. This indicates the subtle fact that each person interprets the same word, situation, or relationship in their own way — a person's understanding functions as per their ability, experiences, and requirements.

Prajapati Brahma's wisdom lies not just in imparting knowledge but also in allowing each descendant to interpret and apply it according to their own cognizance and consciousness. It is a practical and wise learning for all of us. As parents, teachers, mentors, friends, trainers, and leaders, we need to understand that each person will respond to the same teaching and situation differently as per their requirements, awareness, and past experiences. Expecting a similar outcome from everyone is misleading and is likely to to result in poor judgment and conflict. It is an equally relevant learning for business and administrative leaders to be successful. Leaders must be open and accommodative as per the qualities and efficiencies of the workforce associated with the task.

This timeless lesson resonates in every aspect of life, urging us to embrace diversity and adapt our leadership approach to the varied qualities and efficiencies of those under our guidance.

Indeed, as the famous line from the Balkand of the Ramcharitamanas echoes:

जाकीरहीभावनाजैसी,
प्रभुमूरतदेखीतिनतैसी

(The form the Lord assumes is according to the devotee's feelings.)

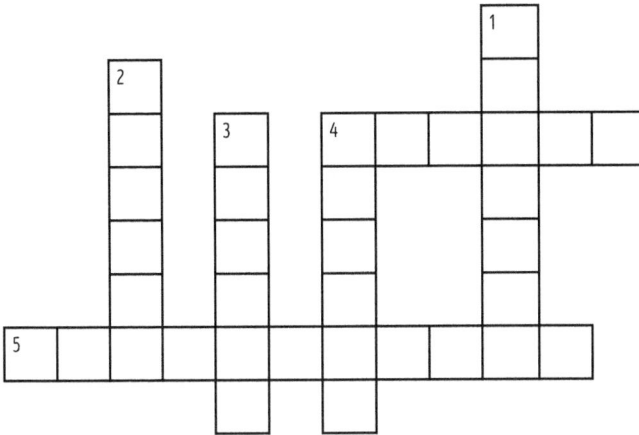

ACROSS

4 One of the Prajapatis

5 The physician of the gods (devas)

DOWN

1 A city in India that is famous for its Brahma Temple and the annual camel festival in the month of Kartik

2 One of the three gunas, associated with goodness, purity, and peace

3 The number of years after which Purna Kumbh is celebrated

4 The descendants of Prajapati who understood his teaching to mean "practice compassion"

14

Agni:
balancing it right

Agni is one of the five elements (*pancha mahabhuta*) combined to form the perceivable material existence. The other four are space (*akash*), water (*jal*), air (*vayu*), and earth (*prithvi*). Fire or *agni* represents heat, desire, and motivation, and it enables transformation. The *panch mahabhutas* are also related to the functioning of the five sensory organs: fire is related to vision or the eyes, air to skin, water to the tongue, space or sky to the ears, and earth to the nose.

Agni is the purifying (*pavaka*) and transformative element. In the Ramayana, it purified Goddess Sita after she returned from Lanka, as she had spent a considerable length of time in the captivity of the asuras. Sita's *agni parikshan* symbolizes the burning away of the negativities arising out of association with unethical and negative people.

In the Yudhisthira and yaksha *samvad* (dialogue) in the Vana Parva of the Mahabharata, the yaksha asks Yudhisthira to answer several questions as a precondition for bringing his dead brothers to life. Two of these questions pertain to Agni. The yaksha asked, "What is the remedy for biting cold?" Yudhisthira replied, "Fire is the remedy for biting cold." At another point, the yaksha questioned, "Who is a welcome guest for everyone?" Yudhisthira replied, "Agni is a welcome guest for everyone."

Sahdeva, Yudhisthira's younger brother, had to take Agni's permission when he wanted to cross the kingdom of Mahismati during Yudhisthira's Rajasuya Yagna. Agni is given the status of an *atithi* (guest) everywhere, except for the domain of Mahismati, where he resides and guards the kingdom for the love of his life, Sudarshana.

Sudarshana was King Nila's daughter, and Agni fell in love with her. However, King Nila did not agree to Agni's proposal for Sudarshana. This refusal upset Agni, who disappeared from King Nila's sacrificial fire. In the absence of fire, no sacrifices or *yagna*, which were essential means to accumulate the merits and power of the king, could be conducted. The king approached the learned sages, and they all tried, but in vain. Finally, King Nila agreed to give his daughter in marriage to Agni but on the condition that Agni would forever stay in Mahismati. So, it was only in the kingdom of Mahismati that Agni dwelled forever; at other places, he had to be invoked, invited, and worshipped to complete the *yagnas* or other rituals.

Out of the numerous stories associated with Agni, one amusing story talks about how Swaha gets close to Agni by disguising herself as the wives of the six *rishis* to lure Agni. Swaha had set her sights on Agni, but Agni was oblivious to this fact. Meanwhile, Agni saw the seven wives of the *saptarshi* (seven sages) during a *yagna* and wanted to possess these seven women of boundless beauty and intellect. However, knowing the power of the *rishis* and that these women were devoted to their husbands, he knew this was impossible. Agni wandered restlessly, thinking about those beauties. Swaha, upon learning of Agni's intentions, disguised herself as the wives of those *rishis* and approached Agni. Agni was pleased each time to see one of the *rishi* wives he had wanted to possess and would accept the proposal of Swaha in disguise. Swaha managed to disguise herself as six of the wives but could not assume the form of Arundhati as she was too pure and powerful. However, when Swaha tried to disguise herself as Arundhati, Agni understood that it was Swaha in disguise each time. Agni accepted Swaha as his wife and stated that any offerings during rituals should be made to Swaha first, and only then would he accept any offer. It is also understood by many that Skanda was the son of Agni and Swaha, and a few believe that he was the son of Shiva and Parvati, born outside the body of Parvati.

↶↷

Agni, a multifaceted, prominent Rigvedic god, has maintained his status through the changing times. The complex nature of Agni has been simplified over time as a few of his features and functions were delegated to others, and a few rituals lost their significance with time. However, Agni still ruled the world with its three levels of presence and as one of the *pancha mahabhuta* that made this world and everything that we perceive. Though many Rigvedic gods assumed lesser positions in the post-Vedic period and some gods were renamed, Agni holds the same significance and diverse nature (since fire is used in various activities, from cooking to lighting the funeral pyre) as in the Vedic period. Agni is commonly perceived as the sacrificial fire and acts as the messenger of gods. Hardly any ritual or *samskara* is performed in the absence of fire.

Agni is one of the oldest gods mentioned in the Rigveda. Rigveda commences with a prayer to Lord Agni:

ॐ अग्निमीळे पुरोहितं यज्ञस्य देवमृत्विजम् ।
होतारं रत्नधातमम् ॥ १.१.१॥

(I praise Agni, who is the priest of the
yagna sacrifice)

Agni, also called the guardian of *rita* (*dharma*),
occupies a prominent position in the Vedas, next
to Lord Indra, in the number of dedicated hymns.
Agni was also a part of the Rigvedic triad of Indra,
Agni, and Surya (sun), existing at three levels. In his
commentary on the Upanishads, Shri Aurobindo
says that Indra, Vayu, and Agni represent the cosmic
Divine on each of the three planes: Indra on the
mental, Vayu on the vital, and Agni on the material.

Numerous stories are related to Agni Deva,
which have their source in the Vedas, Upanishads,
Ramayana, Mahabharata, Brahmans, and Puranas.

Agni Purana, one of the important Puranas, is named after the fire god. It is believed that Lord Agni had revealed the nature of Brahman to Rishi Vashishta, who in turn narrated this to Ved Vyasa, who wrote Agni Purana. Agni also exposed a part of the nature of Brahman to Jabala Satyakam in the Chandogya Upanishad.

Agni is *agrayatvat,* the first in this universe, meaning someone who existed before anyone or anything was created. Agni is *agrani* or the leader. Not limiting to the leader or the first one in the universe, he is also one of the ashta dikpala, the guardians of directions, and the southeast direction is attributed to Agni. Agni is said to exist at three levels: fire on the earth, the sun in the sky, and lightning in the atmosphere. Agni is considered as the messenger of sacrifices offered during *yagnas* to god. Displaying the utmost respect for the feminine divine power, his wife Swaha is addressed first with the offerings to please Lord Agni. Swaha is the *prakriti* and Agni is the *purush,* and their combination completes the sacrificial fire.

Agni is symbolic of the psychological and physiological aspects of life. According to the Maha Puranas, there are three kinds of Agni inside every human being: *krodhagni* or the fire of anger, *kamagni* or the fire of passion and desire, and *udaragni* or the fire of digestion. All three need offerings of forgiveness, detachment, and fasting if one aspires to a harmonious life. Ayurveda further differentiates the metabolic fire of digestion as *jatharagni* (production of hydrochloride acid in the stomach), *bhutagni* (production of bile acids in the liver) and *klomagni* (production of sugar-digesting pancreatic enzymes).

The interpretation and understanding of Agni changed from Vedic to Upanishadic to Puranic times, but its preeminence was never replaced. The essential life-giving *agni* of the universe remained necessary for humans in the form of desire, passion, transformation, purificatory power, and digestive power. Every ritual from birth to death needed the presence of Agni.

The two forms of Agni—Jataveda, which carries the offerings from humans to gods and Kravyada, the Agni of the funeral pyre, which symbolizes transmigration, rebirth, and recycle—have a deep significance for humans. Jataveda is that fire within us that generates the aspiration to be one with the divine and cultivate divine qualities. The power to burn our vices, fears, and weaknesses and keep evolving is the Kravyada fire that transforms us.

Let's keep our inner fire (Agni) alive as it symbolizes inner and outer transformation. As the nature of Agni is to rise above or ascend, we must pray to Lord Agni to help us grow beyond material pursuits and balance our spiritual goals.

Agni maintains his paramount importance in contemporary Hindu practices, playing a central role in various rituals. Serving as a revered purifier, fire acts as the essential conduit through which offerings are made to numerous deities in diverse ceremonies, including *samskaras*, rituals, *havans*, and *yagnas*. From daily household worship to significant life events, fire is indispensable, symbolizing purification and divine connection. Beyond its religious significance, fire holds cultural resonance within Hinduism, being integral to festive celebrations like Diwali and Holi. Additionally, fire serves aesthetic purposes, with lamps and diyas adorning homes and temples for beautification. Lastly, fire plays a crucial role in the final journey of the physical body after death, symbolizing its return to the elemental components from which it originated.

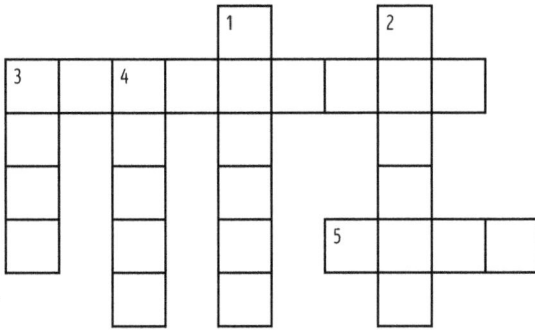

ACROSS

3 The sage to whom Agni revealed the nature of Brahman which was written in Agni Puran by Ved Vyas

5 The god who is believed to stay permanently in the kingdom of Mahishmati

DOWN

1 The Hindu god who is believed to sleep (Yog Nidra) for four months during which no auspicious activities are planned

2 Rishi who cursed Agni to become devourer of all things in the world

3 One of the Panchabhutas along with Agni

4 Daksha's daughter and Agni's wife

Uddalaka to Shvetketu:
Humble heroes have always won the war

The ego and absence of self-awareness have always been among the biggest impediments to the perception of reality. When the mind is preoccupied with the ego, it filters knowledge and information through the lens of personal biases. The ego tends to cling to belief and rigid ideologies, making it difficult for the mind to unlearn and relearn. Controlling the ego has been a topic of mentoring and counseling since antiquity. It has probably existed since humans started staying in social groups. Indian scriptures and folk tales have numerous stories of the excessive egos of gods, kings, ordinary men, and demons engulfing their beholders. Lord Indra, Ravana, Duryodhana, Hiranyakashipu, and Dhana Nanda (who wronged Chanakya) are a few examples from a long list. All these stories point to the philosophy that humble heroes have always won the war. In the Chandogya

Upanishad, a beautiful story of a wise and scholarly
father and a celebrated son finds mention, which
echoes this philosophy.

In keeping with the traditions of the Vedic society,
Uddalaka Aruni, the celebrated wise sage, sent his
son Shvetketu to scholarly Rishi Gautam's *ashram* to
pursue his *brahmacharya ashram*. During his *gurukul*
education, Shvetketu, a bright student, mastered
various subjects like the Vedas, grammar, language,
astronomy, astrology, and so on. He evolved as a
good debater and orator.

During those times, it was a norm for the guru to
take his able students to various debating platforms
to showcase their wisdom and knowledge, bringing
applause and praise for the teacher and the student.
Over time, Shvetketu established his expertise in
those debates, bringing name and fame to his guru
and himself. However, with every win, Shvetketu's
pride swelled.

When the period of his *brahmacharya ashram*
was over, Shvetketu returned to his father's house.
With a sparkle in his eyes, Uddalaka received his
son, who had made him proud with his academic
achievements. However, within a few days,
Uddalaka observed arrogance or ego in Shwetketu.
It is said that "As the sun reveals even the tiniest
shadow, so do parents' eyes uncover every hidden
truth." Uddalaka, the wise sage, knew that arrogance

or *ahamkara* ultimately weakens the personality and restrains the growth of an individual.

He got anxious about his son, who was otherwise an able and competent person. However, he was surrounded by the dark cloud of ego, which would root out his acquired knowledge and obstruct his further pursuit.

After introspecting on the problem, Uddalaka devised a strategy. He wanted a behavioral change in Shvetketu, which was possible only if Shvetketu realized that he needed to change. This process of realization needed the active participation of the student. So, he devised a way to lead Shvetketu to this realization. In didactic strategies, a teacher designs a system and plans to achieve specific learning objectives; similarly, Uddalaka designed a way ahead. He knew that Shvetketu was competent in all other subjects and to make him realize his mistake would be difficult. At the same time, Uddalaka was sure that Shvetketu did not know the essence of the Vedas and had not gathered knowledge about Vedanta. The wise sage knew that a person exposed to Vedanta would be humble and not arrogant. So, he started implmenting his step-wise strategy.

Uddalaka called his son and asked him, "Dear Shvetketu, did you expose yourself to that knowledge by knowing which all is known (the knowledge which is the basis of all other knowledge)? Through

acquiring this knowledge, whatever is unheard becomes heard, whatever is unthought becomes thought, and whatever is unknown becomes known?" Shvetketu responded, "Is there any such knowledge?" He was baffled that he wasn't aware that such knowledge existed. Uddalaka simplified the question and explained it through an example. "Take a lump of gold. We make jewelry, coins, and other objects from gold. But if we melt those objects again, don't they reduce themselves to their earlier form, a lump of gold? This is the material cause. Then there is the goldsmith who makes the objects but is not an object. He does not himself become the object. This is the efficient cause." Uddalaka paused and asked his son, "Does this makes sense to you? Have you been initiated into this kind of knowledge?"

Rather than accepting that he was clueless about such knowledge, Shvetketu replied, "I don't think my teacher knew this, or else he would have told me." This reply strengthened Uddalaka's resolve, and it became all the more necessary to check Shvetketu's ego. Shvetketu wasn't even ready to accept that he didn't know; instead, he said his teacher may not have known.

However, as an ambitious scholar, Shvetketu was by now equally disturbed that he wasn't aware of this higher knowledge. With humility and an awareness of his limitations, he requested his father to expose him to this knowledge. His request initiated a long, intense discourse on Vedanta. One of the most profound teachings that Uddalaka imparted to Shvetketu is the *mahavakya* (great saying) "*Tat tvam asi*" from the Chandogya Upanishad. This *mahavakya* encapsulates the essence of Advaita Vedanta, emphasizing the unity of the individual *atman* (soul) with the ultimate reality (Brahman). Uddalaka used various analogies (like clay and a clay pot) and explanations to convey this non-dualistic truth to Shvetketu, helping him realize the deeper essence of existence.

Gradually, Shvetketu realized that he still had a lot to learn and what he knew was a small part of the limitless ocean of knowledge and wisdom. Those exposed to fundamental knowledge are humble, have no ego, and constantly strive to remove *maya* (illusion) from society. This realization and learning made him humble, and his ego disappeared.

The dialogue between Shvetketu and Uddalaka brings to the surface a sharp distinction between mastering the academic curriculum or academic success versus education, which leads to character building. Mere knowledge or information about values is not enough; it must reflect in the knower's attitude and behavior.

Parenting has always been challenging, with no concrete model to follow and no universal rules to guarantee success. While different yardsticks may define success, the importance of shaping a good human being and building character has been unquestioned since ancient times. No amount of academic or professional success can sustain itself if the person achieving it lacks a strong moral and ethical foundation and self-awareness.

Uddalaka's role in his son's life exemplifies the ideal of parental involvement as a mentor in the holistic development of a child. Through a combination of formal education, personal guidance, and profound spiritual teaching, Uddalaka helped shape Shvetketu's intellectual and spiritual growth. His efforts highlight the significance of wisdom, humility, and the pursuit of deep understanding throughout life's journey.

Uddalaka served as a role model for Shvetketu through his own conduct, demonstrating the importance of parents maintaining a high standard of personal behavior, as children are more likely to emulate what they see rather than what they are told. This story is also important for teachers and mentors, showcasing how Uddalaka taught complex knowledge using simple yet powerful analogies. For instance, he explained the nature of *Brahman* through the analogy of clay and pots, where all pots, despite their different forms, are essentially made of the same clay.

Even though Shvetketu was the celebrated student of his *gurukul*, his father realized that celebrating superficial glory would be detrimental to the child's future. The story of Uddalaka and Shvetketu reminds us that true success lies in the development of a well-rounded character, guided by wisdom and ethical principles.

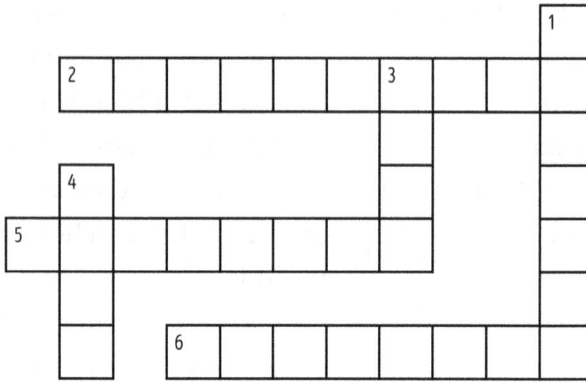

ACROSS

2 The famous mahavakya from Chandogya Upanishad

5 The famous Mahavakya "prajnanam Brahman" meaning "consciousness is the absolute (Brahman)" is from which upanishad

6 Shortest Upanishad

DOWN

1 One of the six major astik (thesitic) schools of Vedic philosophy founded by Jaimini

3 The face or veil that creates the cosmic illusion, presenting phenomenal world to the real according to Advaita Vedanta

4 Hiranyakashipu's mother

16

Look here, look there, you will find them everywhere: Dikpala guarding us all the way

Directions hold great symbolic and spiritual significance in Hindu cosmology and are integral to various religious practices, rituals, house and temple constructions, and daily routines. Directions determine the flow of energy and are divine and holy. Energy is an essential aspect of the spiritual and physical sciences. The sacredness of directions is further intensified by appointing guards for each direction.

In the Vedic and post-Vedic periods, a ruling deity would guard and guide each direction. The gods of the directions were probably responsible for safeguarding or assisting the cosmic order or *rita*, which maintained the physical and moral order of the universe. During the Vedic period, Adityas born out of Aditi were the rulers of the sky, responsible for guarding end to end.

The term *dikpala* or *lokpala* is generally understood in Hinduism to mean the lord of directions. The shift to eight directions from the basic four cardinal directions was seen during the post-Vedic period. In the post-Vedic period emerged a demarcated concept of *ashta dikpala*—guardians who ruled the eight quarters or the eight directions of the universe. *Ashta* means eight, *dik* means quarters or directions, and *pala* means a ruler or one who sustains us. Many prime Vedic gods were identified as *ashta dikpalas* in the post-Vedic period.

It is understood that the idea of guardians of the directions or eight *dikpalas* originated in one of the Puranas, a shift from the earlier belief of guardian gods of four cardinal directions only. There developed more additions and variations of *ashta dikpala* in the form of *dasa dikpala*—the guardians of ten directions or *nava dikpala*—the guardians of nine directions.

Right from the Vedic period to modern times, the belief in the sacredness of directions continued. During the Vedic period, for the various *yagnas* and sacrificial rituals related to *samskaras*, directions and orientation of the sacrifice altar played a vital role. Even in astrology, architecture and daily rituals like *atmapradakshina*—revolving on one's axis in a clockwise direction in front of deities or in a temple—or *pradakshina*—clockwise circumambulation of a temple or sacred entities—the concept of the sacredness of directions prevails. During *atmap-radakshina* or *pradakshina,* along with respecting the self, we also pay respect to our guardian deities in all directions. Even today, architecture takes into consideration the Vastu of the design. Vasthu-shāstra focuses on the directions while designing different structures.

With the significance and sacredness of directions came the demerits of not following the laws of directions. *Dishashul* and *vastu dosha* are two *doshas* (faults or defects) associated with rules of directions that people want to avoid today as well.

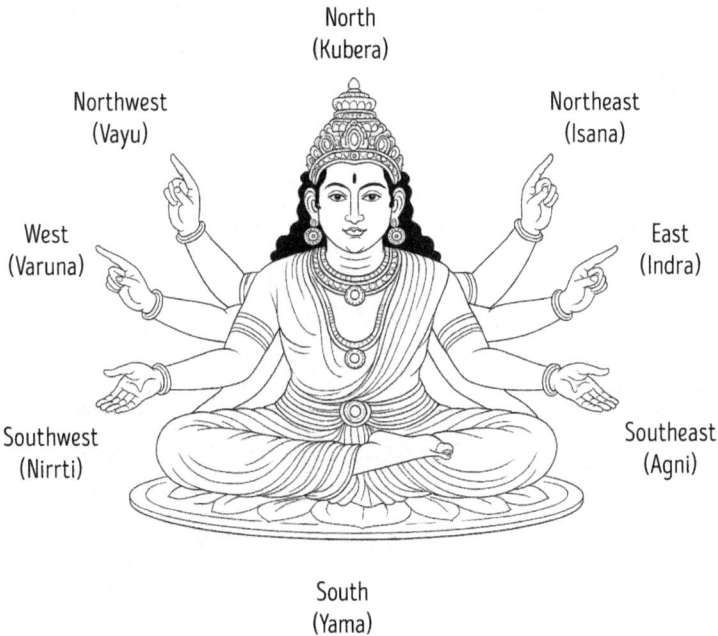

North
(Kubera)

Northwest
(Vayu)

Northeast
(Isana)

West
(Varuna)

East
(Indra)

Southwest
(Nirrti)

Southeast
(Agni)

South
(Yama)

Dishashul is the direction in which one should avoid traveling on particular days, especially if one is undertaking a journey for important or auspicious work. In such cases, people refer to the *panchang* or consult a *purohit* (astrologer or priest). However, if travel is unavoidable, astrological priests can provide a solution. Similarly, to avoid *vastu dosha* or demerits arising from noncompliance with direction and orientation rules while constructing a house, office, temple, or other buildings, even modern architects keep *vastu* principles in mind.

As mentioned earlier, the sacredness of directions and belief in the guardians or gods of directions are crucial in nearly all ancient religions with their own gods or demigods. Ancient Javanese and Bali Hinduism recognize *nava dikpala*, guardians of nine directions—eight directions with one addition in the center. Hinduism spread to the Indonesian archipelago during the first century A.D. when Indian sailors, traders, priests, and scholars started traveling to Indonesia and Bali. A syncretic fusion of preexisting Javanese folk religion and culture with Hindu culture and religious ideas led to the Balinese Hinduism also called *Agma Hindu dharma*. Buddhism (especially Vajrayana Buddhism) and Jainism also believe in *dikpala*. The Chinese have a similar belief in four spirits or guards guarding the four directions: the Azure Dragon of the east, the Vermilion Bird of

the south, the White Tiger of the west, and the Black
Tortoise or Black Warrior of the north. The Greek
god Anemoi were the wind gods, and each wind god
was ascribed a direction.

In the Udyoga Parva of the Mahabharata and
in the Ramayana as well, we find references to the
direction guardians. The Mahabharata mentions
four heavenly quarters guarded or supported by the
guardian cow goddesses Kamadhenu and her four
daughters. The four daughters of Kamadhenu are
Dhenu for the north, Harshika or Hansika for the
south, Saurabhi or Surupa for the east, and Subhadra
for the west. The Ramayana mentions four elephants
who guard the four corners: Virupaksha for the east,
Maha-padma for the south, Saumanas for the west,
and Bhadra for the north. This description resembles
the story of eight elephants that guard the eight
directions. The Brahamanda Purana talks about eight
legendary elephants as the guardians of the eight
directions in Hindu cosmology. In some versions, the
eight elephants are also considered as the vehicles of
eight *dikpalas*.

It is understood that four main deities were
associated with the four cardinal directions — north,
south, west, and east. Later, four more gods were
added to include guardians for the southwest,
southeast, northwest, and northeast, leading to *ashta
dikpala* and *ashta diggaja*.

The commonly accepted *ashta dikpala* since post-Vedic times are Indra, the god of rain and thunder, guarding the eastern quarter; Kubera, the treasurer of Lakshmi, as the guardian of the north; Varuna, the god of water and the sea, guards the western quarters; and Yama, the God of death, guards the southern direction. In addition, Agni, the god of fire, guards the southeastern direction and is next to Indra in importance in the Rigveda. Nirrti represents poverty and corruption and guards the southwestern direction. Vayu, the lord of winds, guards the northwestern quarters and is also mentioned in the Rigveda. Isana, a form of Lord Shiva, represents knowledge and prosperity and guards the northeast direction. All these gods, except Kubera and Isana, appear in the Rigveda.

There were two more additions in some descriptions: Lord Brahma, the creator, represents the zenith or the upward direction (between the northeast and north directions), and Lord Vishnu, the sustainer, represents the nadir (between the southwest and south directions) or the downward direction.

The belief in *dikpalas*, guardians of directions, beautifully symbolizes the omniscience of God, intertwined with rituals, personal deities, and cosmic order. These guardian deities assure a peaceful and prosperous existence by maintaining universal harmony. As we progress scientifically, the belief in religion and spirituality also increases. The fear of the unknown persists, and to counter that, we turn to religion, which offers hope and positivity. Belief in *dikpalas* – that we are being guarded by the direction gods against unseen evil forces – has been a source of solace from ancient times.

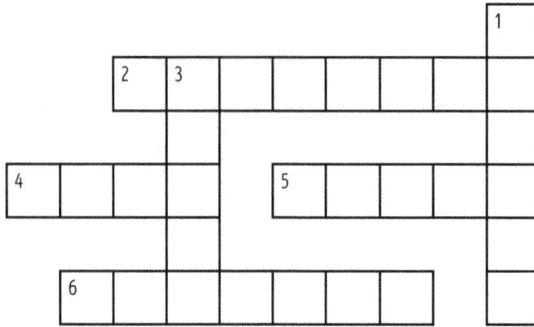

ACROSS

2 Sanskrit treatise on ancient Indian architecture and design

4 The guardian of the southeast direction

5 Kamadhenu's daughter who guards the north direction

6 One common name for these 12 gods: Vivasvan, Aryaman, Tvashta, Savitr, Bhaga, Data, Mitra, Varuna, Amsa, Pushan, Indra, and Vishnu (Vamana form)

DOWN

1 The dikpala who rides a crocodile

3 Mother of the Adityas

17

The sagacious dialogue:
Lord Rama and Kevat

Inclusivity has been embedded in the Indian philosophical, religious, and social fabric and is one of the foundational principles of Indian society. Indian philosophical and religious thought has constantly championed values such as *karuna* (compassion), *bandhutva* (fraternity), *samarasta* (harmony), *swatantrata* (liberty), *swaraj* (self-rule), *vasudhev kutumbakam* (the world is one family), *sarve bhavantu sukhinah* (may all beings be happy), *atithi devo bhava* (your guest is like a god), and *seva* (selfless service) that underscore the essence of an inclusive society.

The *dasavatara* of Vishnu (the ten incarnations of Lord Vishnu), the Ardhanarishwar and Mohini forms of Shiva and Vishnu respectively, the association of various animals and trees with divinity, the portrayal of deities like Lord Jagannatha without limbs, the sacredness of Harihara, who is born out of Vishnu

and Shiva, and the significance of Jatayu in the
Ramayana further exemplify inclusivity in Indian
narratives from time immemorial. The Ramayana,
celebrated for portraying a socially inclusive society,
is a testament to India's enduring commitment
to inclusivity.

The famous *Kevat samvad* of the Ramayana is
discussed in the light of the utter devotion of a
disciple to his lord. The narrative also symbolizes
the inclusivity that was natural to the society of
that period. Kevat (boatman) was an ardent disciple
of Lord Rama. One day, when he unexpectedly
encountered Lord Rama, he was quick to resolve that
he would not let this once-in-a-lifetime opportunity
go in vain. He was determined to seek the blessings
of the Lord by physically touching and washing the
feet of Lord Rama (a gesture of deep respect). Apart
from the narrative exposing us to inclusive society
and devotion, there was a striking facet of this clever
Kevat—his quick-wittedness and intuitiveness,
which he reveals in the dialogue.

The situation goes like this: After being banished
from the kingdom for 14 years, Lord Rama, Devi Sita,
and Rama's younger brother, Lakshmana, proceed
to the jungle. Though the people of Ayodhya, King
Dasharatha, ministers, and advisers tried to stop
him, Lord Rama resolved to go ahead with 14 years
of exile.

Leaving the limits of the capital city behind, Rama, Sita, and Lakshmana arrived at the outskirts of Shringaverpur, a small tribal area governed by Nishad Raj Guha, an old acquaintance of Rama. When Nishad Raj heard about the arrival of the princes of Ayodhya, he eagerly came to meet Rama. After extending his hospitality to Lord Rama, Nishad Raj requested him to spend the rest of his years of exile in his area so that Nishad would benefit from his company and also get to take care of and host him. However, Lord Rama, an embodiment of *dharma*, politely declined the invitation, saying it was against the principles of *vanvaas* (exile in the forest) to seek comfort and care from someone and he would have to go deep into the jungle and stay on his own.

After spending a day there under a tree, Lord Rama requested for a boat to cross the river Ganges to go deep into the forest. Nishad Raj called for the Kevat near the river bank. When they reached, the Kevat recognized Lord Rama. He realized this was a divine opportunity to wash Lord Rama's feet and seek that water as a prasad (offering of the god). Kevat, high in intuitive knowledge, knew that Prince Rama was an incarnation of Lord Vishnu. He started thinking of ways to ensure that he could wash the lord's feet because if he were to ask to do so, the humble Lord Rama might deny his request.

To fulfill his desire, the boatman put a condition

of washing Lord Rama's feet before taking him across in the boat. The reason that he gave compelled Lord Rama to agree to his condition with a smile. This demonstrates the cleverness, intuitiveness, and quick-wittedness of Kevat.

Lord Rama asked Kevat to ferry him across the river. The boatman reluctantly said that Lord Rama's secret magical powers were well known, and people claimed that even the dust of Rama's feet could transform any non-living object into a human being. Conveying his concerns and fears, he recounted the tale of a stone that turned into a beautiful woman, Ahilya, upon touching the divine feet of Lord Rama. Kevat cleverly likened his boat, made of soft wood, to the stone, fearing that it might transform into a woman upon contact with the sacred feet.

The boatman says, "Sir, this boat is my only source

of livelihood. If the dust of your feet changes it into a woman, then how will I earn my living, and how will I ferry you to the other side?"

Impressed by his astuteness, Lord Rama said, "Kevat, please do what it takes to save your boat from transforming into something undesirable and then ferry the three of us across the river." Kevat, without wasting a moment, sprang into action and washed the feet of Lord Rama with utmost affection and devotion. He then respectfully asked the three of them to be seated in his boat.

Upon reaching the other side, Lord Rama, overwhelmed by Kevat's selflessness and wisdom, expressed his desire to repay him for his services. Devi Sita took out the gold ring on her finger, which Lord Rama offered to Kevat. Once again displaying his wisdom, Kevat humbly declined the offering, recognizing the priceless experience of washing the feet of the divine in human form. He said that even the most revered sages and kings would not get this opportunity and he need not be repaid for his services. He stated that he had enough money to take care of his family. The insightful Kevat understood the difference between material gain and spiritual bliss, which even the most learned people do not always understand.

With a heart full of contentment and blessings, Kevat uttered words of gratitude, "I have received everything today. Your blessings are all I need to overcome any adversity. I promise that on your return journey, I will not refuse any gift you want to give me."

So, with their hearts full of mutual respect and admiration, the boatman and the divine parted ways, each enriched by the encounter.

Lord Rama, who helps individuals cross the ocean of this life and whose blessings have the power to free the individual from the bondage of the karmic cycle, humbly accepted the conditions laid by the boatman. Rama is all-embracing. He knows no difference between people based on their caste, social status, or gender. Lord Rama's life and principles have social inclusion embedded in them.

When there is worldwide discussion on making our societies inclusive, we need to take a leaf out of the Ramayana.

मागी नाव न केवटु आना । कहइ तुम्हार मरमु मैं जाना ॥
चरन कमल रज कहुँ सबु कहई । मानुष करनि मूरि कछु अहई ॥2॥

छुअत सिला भइ नारि सुहाई । पाहन तें न काठ कठिनाई ॥
तरनिउ मुनि घरिनी होइ जाई । बाट परइ मोरि नाव उड़ाई ॥3॥

एहिं प्रतिपालउँ सबु परिवारू । नहिं जानउँ कछु अउर कबारू ॥
जौं प्रभु पार अवसि गा चहहू । मोहि पद पदुम पखारन कहहू ॥4॥

कृपासिंधु बोले मुसुकाई । सोइ करु जेहिं तव नाव न जाई ॥
बेगि आनु जलपाय पखारू । होत बिलंबु उतारहि पारू ॥1॥

नाथ आजु मैं काह न पावा । मिटे दोष दुख दारिद दावा ॥
बहुत काल मैं कीन्हि मजूरी । आजु दीन्ह बिधि बनि भलि भूरी ॥3॥

अब कछु नाथ न चाहिअ मोरें । दीन दयाल अनुग्रह तोरें ॥
फिरती बार मोहि जो देबा । सो प्रसादु मैं सिर धरि लेबा ॥4॥

This famous dialogue between Kevat and Lord
Rama beautifully expresses Kevat's devotion, along
with his cleverness, intuitiveness, quick-wittedness,
and sense of purpose, which deserve emulation by
one and all. Kevat demonstrates that if our resolution
is firmly winged with the power of good insight,
wisdom, and wit, even God responds.

Kevat's wisdom in discerning between spiritual
fulfillment and material gain is a profound example
for all. The story serves as a timeless reminder of
the importance of inclusivity in societal harmony
and individual conduct, inspiring emulation and
reflection in contemporary contexts.

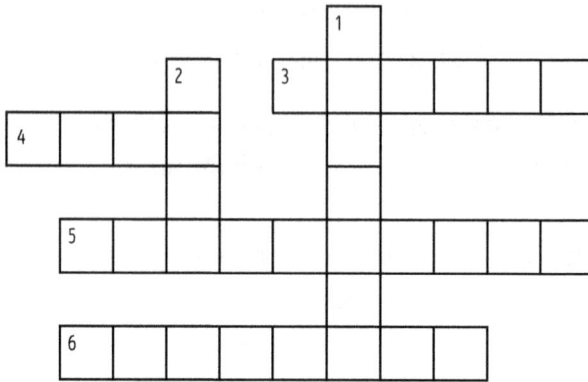

ACROSS

3 The sage who was Sabri's guru, and prophesied that Rama would visit her in the ashram one day

4 The architect of Ram Setu to Lanka, who is also known to be Lord Vishwakarma's son

5 The forest area where Rama, Lakshmana, and Sita spent the initial years of exile; the famous place where Bharata, upon hearing of Rama's exile, came to meet him and request him to return to Ayodhya

6 King Janak's wife and Sita's mother

DOWN

1 The famous sage who was Ahilya's husband and cursed her to turn into a stone

2 The demon king for whom Bali Pratipada is celebrated

18

Embracing impermanence:
Kubera's rise to divinity

As a way of life, Hinduism unfolds profound life philosophies by embodying them through a pantheon of divinity and divine human beings. Within this spiritual tapestry, the absence of double standards becomes evident, where a common set of principles applies to demons, deities, and humans, all bearing the inherent constraints of their respective birthplaces and planes of existence. In the diverse shades of Hindu philosophy, a core tenet—the impermanence of all things—offers hope and inspiration. This foundational belief signifies that transformation is accessible to everyone, regardless of whether we stand among the divine, the demoniacal, or the human.

Throughout Hindu lore, there are numerous compelling instances of individuals, be they humans or demons, ascending to god-like status through unwavering dedication and exceptional practice.

Conversely, these narratives also reveal gods who
have fallen from their divine pedestals because of a
wavering commitment to *dharma* and the allure of
unguarded desires and indulgences. According to a
legend, Kubera was driven out of Lanka by his half-brother, Ravana, and even
his Pushpak Vimana, gifted to him by Lord Indra,
was stolen by Ravana. Faced with such extreme
life challenges and with nowhere to go, Kubera
proceeded to Mount Kailasha, where he underwent
deep meditation and austerity. Moved by his
penance, Lord Shiva blessed him with his company
and eventually the the status of a demigod.

Kubera then went on to build the beautiful city of
Alaka (Alkapuri), and his heavenly garden, Caitharth,
was frequented by several gods, including Lord
Shiva and Goddess Parvati. After his association with
Shiva and Parvati grew, he also became associated
with Goddess Lakshmi, the goddess of fortune and
auspiciousness. Many believe that Goddess Lakshmi
appointed him as treasurer for material wealth
while she was the superior goddess of fortune and
auspiciousness. For all kinds of material wealth,
Kubera started being associated with Lakshmi, who
was much more than the goddess of material wealth.

Initially, Kubera was not recognized as a god in
the Vedic period. He is one of the gods who is an
example of transformation, from guhayaka or yaksha

to god. He gradually acquired divinity but was not born with it. There were major transformations in the names and nature of Kubera between the Vedic and Puranic periods. Initially, he was referred to as Guhayakadhipati (Lord of Guhayakas), Yakshadhipati (king of yakshas), Nara or Vahana (one who rides on spirits or humans), or Bhutesha (king of spirits). He was also known as Ekaksipingala (one with one yellow eye) after Goddess Parvati cursed him when he secretly observed her and Lord Shiva spending private time together. He is also called Yaksharajan (king of yakshas) and Kinnara Raja (lord of kinnaras). In the Atharvaveda, he is mentioned as the chief of the spirit of darkness. The *Shatapatha Brahmana* calls him the lord of thieves and criminals.

He was acknowledged as the king of yakshas in major Indian-origin religions like Hinduism, Buddhism, and Jainism. In Jainism, he was the attendant yaksha of the 19th Tirthankara, Mallinatha. In Buddhism, Kubera is called Vaisravana, and like the Hindu Kubera, his position was restricted to lord of the yakshas, who was the regent of the North, a *lokpala*. However, by the time of the Puranas and epics, Kubera had acquired the higher status of a god.

The Puranas, the Mahabharata, and the Ramayana granted Kubera godhood. Apart from being a *lokpala*, he also aquired the status of Dhanadhipati (lord of wealth) and Rajaraja (king of kings), probably because he controlled the world's material riches after his association with other divine entities and Goddess Lakshmi. With time, he became one of the revered gods in Hinduism, Jainism, and Buddhism. He assumed a stronger position as a *dikpala* or *lokpala*, the guardian of the north direction, along with possessing other powers, like controlling the wealth of the world. In the Ramayana, he is mentioned as the god of gold and wealth.

As the wealthiest god, Dhanadhipati, a story associates him with Tirupati Balaji temple. It is believed that Lord Kubera lent money to Lord Vishnu's incarnation, Shrinivas, so that he could marry Padmavati (an incarnation of Goddess Lakshmi), the daughter of the king of seven hills.

Shrinivas (Lord Venkateshwara), born into a humble family, fell in love with Princess Padmavati. The girl's father, however, demanded a massive sum of money for marriage. Shrinivas, Lord Vishnu's incarnation, approached Lord Kubera for a loan of the same amount. The loan amount was so huge that Shrinivas could not repay it quickly. The devotees of Tirupati Balaji temple are still helping Lord Vishnu (incarnated as Shrinivas) repay the loan through their donations to the Tirupati temple. Lord Venkateshwara is believed to stay in the hills of Tirumala (where the Tirupati temple is situated) until the loan is repaid. As per the belief, the loan amount gets repaid at the end of Kaliyug.

Hinduism applauds coexistence and inclusivity between gods, demons, humans, and ecology. This story of Kubera lending money to Shrinivas and Padmavati offers an insight into the philosophy of coexistence. It reflects life's undeniable truth; interdependence for existence. When even the divine seek the collective help of humanity to fulfill their purpose, then to think of ourselves as invincible is akin to insanity.

The story of Lord Kubera unveils a profound truth about the changing nature of situations and roles. Kubera's journey is a testament to the transformative power that resides in every individual. He progressed remarkably from the leadership of evil spirits to the throne of the yakshas, ultimately achieving divine status.

The story of Lord Kubera resounds with a deep-rooted philosophy: It acknowledges the impermanence that underlies all aspects of existence. It reminds us that every role can change and every soul can evolve toward more incredible spiritual and emotional refinement. The story brings the profound message home that in embracing impermanence, we find hope, not despair. It is a reminder that there are no fixed compartments or immovable barriers in life. Our existence in this world offers us many opportunities, an invitation to break free from the limitations that bind us and evolve to higher realms of understanding. Embracing inherent impermanence is the key to higher spiritual and intellectual planes.

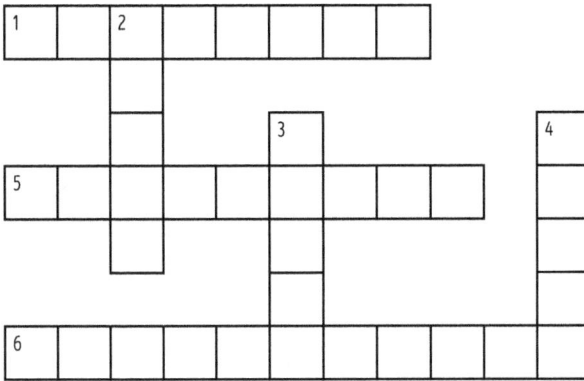

ACROSS

1 The abode of Kubera
5 The serpent associated with Lord Vishnu
6 Kubera's friend, a gandharva, who stopped Arjuna from touching the waters of the Bhagirathi

DOWN

2 The god who is also known as Ekaksipingala, meaning one who has one yellow eye
3 The god who gifted Pushpak Vimana to Kubera
4 The god whose celestial bow is called Pinaka

Draupadi and Satyabhama's conversation:
Quest for a blessed relationship

Of the several women characters in the Mahabharata, Draupadi was different. She exercised her rights when needed and diligently executed her duties. She was forgiving as well as vengeful. Born out of a *yagna* fire, she was also known as Yagnaseni. Panchali (another name for Draupadi) was one of the main protagonists whose actions and presence led to decisive moments in the Mahabharata. She counseled and guided the Pandavas on various occasions. A friend of Krishna and respectfully trusted by the Pandava brothers, she had a significant presence in their personal and professional lives.

Women have the same core desires when it comes to relationships. The marital relationship, then and now, works on the same fundamental principles of transparency, trust, dependability, respect, and mutual growth. The questions that Satyabhama, the

warrior wife of Krishna, asked Draupadi about the
marital relationship are often discussed today with
marriage counselors, friends, and well-wishers:
How do you keep the respect and love alive in the
relationship? What does it take for a woman to
command respect and obedience from her husband?
A similar set of questions arises on the men's side
as each person, regardless of gender, desires a
harmonious and fulfilling relationship.

Draupadi and Satyabhama's dialogue in the
Vana Parva of the Mahabharata dwells on the core
issues of relationships. Satyabhama asks Draupadi,
"O beautiful lady, what do you do that your
husbands—handsome, young, able warriors, who
are themselves like *lokpalas*—are obedient to you and
never get angry with you?" Satyabhama wants to
know whether Draupadi uses any tricks or sorcery

or administers any drug to her husbands so that they submit to Draupadi. She asks whether Draupadi knows any *homa* (sacrifice) that results in obedient and admiring husbands.

Draupadi's reply is very progressive and holistic, as if coming from an experienced psychologist. The role of women has changed drastically from those times, but the answer remains relevant to modern relationships.

In reply to Satyabhama, Draupadi says that tricks, sorcery, drugs, and *homa* to control the husband are the work of wicked women, and she does not know anything about them. If a man finds out that his wife uses such practices to earn her husband's respect or love or to tame him, he becomes fearful of the effects of those practices, and fear leads to the absence of peace and happiness. Draupadi states that neither does she know the ways of wicked women nor do these tricks work.

The Adi Parva of the Mahabharata describes the unparalleled beauty of Draupadi. The dark complexioned, fire-born beauty had large eyes like a lotus petal. She had a slender waist and a deep bosom. Her body exuded the fragrance of a blue lotus, perceivable from a long distance. Like a celestial herself, she was desired in marriage by the divine, danavas and yakshas.

Despite being among the most beautiful women,

Draupadi does not attribute the respect and love she gets from her husbands to her physical beauty. The Pandavas were enchanted not by her beauty, but by her conduct and selfless service, intelligence, and competence to manage the vast Pandava empire.

Draupadi further says that proper conduct was the only reason that the Pandavas respected her. Abandoning jealousy and vanity, being alert to the needs of people who depended on her, and being attentive like a wife and queen to the needs of her husbands and subjects were the attributes that set her apart from other women. Draupadi believed that a woman should be the best confidant of her husband and vice versa. She should not share with anyone the secrets her husband confides in her.

Elaborating on her daily routine, she says that she was the first to leave the bed and the last one to retire. She ate once all family members, Brahmins, and other guests had eaten. "Others before self" is the principle she followed.

She further says that when the Pandavas lived in Indraprastha, they had one hundred thousand maidservants, well versed in dancing and singing. Draupadi personally knew them; she knew what they ate and what they were good at. One lakh horses and one lakh elephants followed Yudhisthira when he ruled. Draupadi knew the exact location and numbers and was aware of those who managed those elephants and horses. While the Pandavas were busy in the pursuit of *dharma*, it was she who managed the finances and looked after the treasury of the kingdom.

Draupadi had an unforgiving nature and a thirst for vengeance. Following their exile in the forest, she repeatedly questioned Yudhisthira's integrity, even likening his apparent calmness to cowardice. She constantly urged him, his brothers, and their allies to wage war against the Kauravas. Her relentless interrogation agitated even Bhima, who joined her in challenging Yudhisthira about following the conditions of the unjust and deceitful game of dice.

Draupadi's desire for retribution against the Kauravas was palpable, yet it was Yudhisthira who presented reasoned arguments for adhering to the prescribed period of exile and seeking the return of their rightful kingdom and wealth. He proposed that they should patiently complete their punishment and only resort to war if the Kauravas refused to rectify their wrongdoing.

Draupadi could make decisions for herself. In the past, she had decided for herself and defied societal expectations by having five husbands. Opting to accompany the Pandavas during their twelve years of forest exile and the subsequent one year of *agyatvas* (living in disguise or anonymity), she purposefully took on the role of a hairdresser and maid to a queen.

Although the exile was not obligatory for her, she willingly embraced it, recognizing the importance of standing in solidarity with her husbands.

She understood that proximity nurtures understanding and solidarity and consciously chose to stand by the Pandavas. In doing so, she not only asserted her autonomy but also embodied the essence of true companionship, accepting their challenges and punishments as her own. Through her actions, she exemplified the essence of companionship, demonstrating the strength of unity and mutual support

Draupadi rescued and ensured freedom for the Pandavas from slavery after they lost in the game of dice. After Duryodhana and Dushasana attempted to disrobe Draupadi, she was about to curse the entire Kuru clan. However, Dhritarashtra, counseled by Gandhari, offered three boons to Panchali to appease her and cover up his sons' sins. Draupadi redeemed only two boons by first asking for her husbands' freedom from slavery so that her sons would not be called sons of slaves. For the second boon, she asked that all the wealth Yudhisthira had lost in the game be restored to him. She did not display greed by using the third boon. Draupadi was the savior for her husbands. She showed the way to have an equal relationship. In a relationship of equals, not only are husbands supposed to save and protect their wives from difficult situations, but wives can also do the same for their husbands.

Draupadi says that this pressure of holding the support system of an empire and a large family cannot be borne by a woman who has an evil heart. Only someone who keeps their heart free of negative feelings can handle this load. "This is the charm that I have used to make my husbands obedient, and there are no other tricks I know," says Draupadi to Satyabhama.

Hearing this, Satyabhama, the incarnation of Bhudevi (the earth goddess) was full of reverence for Panchali, and she blessed her to be free from fear and grief in her life. Satyabhama further said that a person with such a pure heart could never suffer misfortune for long and gave her blessings to Panchali and her husbands for regaining what rightfully belonged to them.

Draupadi, though a woman who was known to make extraordinary choices in life, did get deterred like an ordinary person by the humiliation and deprivation she suffered. That was the reason she relentlessly questioned Yudhisthira's acceptance of exile. However, she used that humiliation to empower herself and keep the fire of vengeance alive in the Pandavas' hearts. At the same time, she was also resilient. She was outspoken and made herself heard whenever she was wronged. She even questioned her eldest husband when he staked her in the game of dice.

Marriage has always been sacrosanct in Hindu tradition. Being one of the essential *samskaras* or rites of passage, marriage is revered and is believed to bring completeness to a man, the wife being his *ardhangini* or the other half in Hindu *shastras* as a *griha patni, dharma patni,* and *sahdharmini*. Apart from the various ways in which the relationship was defined in the scriptures, what remained in essence is a suggestion for a harmonious and equal relationship.

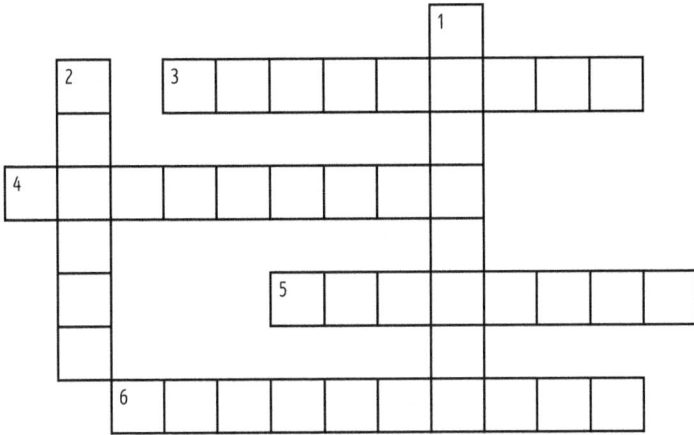

ACROSS

3 Kamdev's incarnation, born out of Krishna and one of his chief consorts, Rukmini

4 A Yadav king and Satyabhama's father

5 In one year of living in disguise, Draupadi became the hairdresser (*sairandhri*) to this queen

6 Lord Krishna's wife, who helped him fight against the demon Narkasur

DOWN

1 Arjuna's name because of his curly hair and because he had conquered sleep

2 One of the *purnimas* on which Lord Krishna is believed to have performed the famous *maharaas*

Partnering for life:
Starry tales from Arundhati-Vashishtha and Dhruv tara

Folk tales are fluid, and they have an inherent intelligence. They are carriers of traditions and rituals and keep the culture flowing. However, each of these rituals and interpretations has regional variations. These stories are traveling metaphors that assume new meanings in different regions depending on what society wants to propagate or its cultural aspirations.

The story of Arundhati and Vashishtha, and that of Dhruv tara, are two such stories that have scientific intelligence and cultural aspirations embedded in them. Cultural aspirations are reflected in the qualities these stories consider significant for relationships or partnerships, such as consistency, dependency, and mutual growth. These attributes find high emotional aspiration in the context of a partnership or marriage.

Arundhati
  . .   .
     Vasistha   Dhruv

There is a ritual of showing the binary stars of
Arundhati and Vashishtha and Dhruv *tara* in many
Indian marriages. In doing so, hope and blessings
are given to the newlyweds that they should aspire
for a relationship as equal and supportive as that
of Arundhati and Vashishtha and as constant and
guiding as Dhruv *tara*.

A relationship must be well-coordinated (like
a binary star system) where one person is not the
system's center. It is a partnership, and for any
alliance to be at its optimum efficiency, both the
parties need to contribute and mutually benefit as
individuals. Modern researchers have also pointed
to the mental and physical health benefits of having
a compatible spouse who shares similar values and

priorities because such a relationship accelerates individual growth and team growth.

Modern relationship counselors reiterate the need to help each other in the process of self-discovery and growth. There are various such examples in ancient stories. Ubheya Bharati helped Madan Mishra, her husband, assume the role of a hermit after he was defeated by Adi Shankaracharya in a debate where she was the moderator, which is an exemplary role of a partner. Similarly, during one of the discourses of Vashishtha, Arundhati stepped up and sought his permission to take the teachings ahead for his students. Vashishtha was taken aback by her clear perception of the subject. Overwhelmed, he said to Arundhati, "You are my *ardhangini* — wife or other half — in the true sense."

After the rituals in most Indian marriages, the bride and bridegroom are shown the Polaris star (Dhruv *tara*) and the binary stars, Alcor and Mizar (Arundhati and Vashishtha). There is a beautiful logic behind why only these stars, and no other stars, are shown.

Alcor and Mizar (part of the Ursa Major constellation) are the only binary stars in the celestial world that are gravitationally bound and co-orbit. It signifies an equal relationship where one is not the center and the other orbits around it, but both are centers for each other. For a marriage or alliance to be fulfilling and compatible, it requires balancing and complementing each other's skill sets and strengths, just as Arundhati and Vashishtha hold each other.

Dhruv *tara* or Polaris or pole star is part of the Ursa Minor constellation. It is known as the dependable star and is constant to its position in the sky. It has been acting as the compass for human travelers since antiquity. In most Indian marriages, after the marriage ritual gets over in the wee hours, the newlyweds are shown this star. There are various locally sung marriage songs where seeing Dhruv *tara* is mentioned; for example, "देखो देखो ध्रुवतारा, ध्रुवतारे सा हो अमर सुहाग तिहारा, देखो देखो ध्रुवतारा" (The couple is asked to look at Dhruv *tara* and is being blessed to have an immortal marriage. The couple seeks blessings that their relationship remains as unshakable and constant as Dhruv *tara*).

Dhruv means unshakable, unmovable, and fixed. Similarly, our relationship, marriage, or alliance should be steady and fixed. Dhruv has been the guiding light for navigators; likewise, life partners should guide each other even on the darkest of nights.

Dhruv is not the brightest star in the sky, but it is the most dependable. Similarly, individuals in a marriage or relationship need not be extrinsically beautiful, but they must have tenacity and dependability.

The stories of both Arundhati–Vashishtha and Dhruv have been wonderfully woven in our folktales and have an unquestionable scientific basis (the co-orbiting of Arundhati and Vashishtha and the stable position of Dhruv *tara*). They are used to counsel newlyweds for a balanced and fulfilling relationship.

Arundhati, the wife of Vashishtha, was a learned, unblemished, inspiring, and exemplary woman. Her learning and strength of character were so superior that she could not be impersonated even by Swaha, who wanted to captivate Agni by emulating the wives of the saptarshi (seven sages). Swaha could impersonate the wives of six of the seven sages, but not Arundhati. According to another story, Arundhati had excellent counseling skills, which she used to convince Lord Shiva to marry Parvati.

Arundhati (Alcor) is a fainter star as compared to Vashishtha (Mizar) and is identified in the sky after Vashishtha is visible — the star's position is identified relative to the position of Vashishtha. There is great learning here as well. Even if one of the partners is easily identified because they shine in the outer world, their brightness and shine will always point to the partner who contributes to holding them together with their qualities and skill sets.

Dhruv's story is one of perseverance and courage. The child Dhruv set out to seek Lord Vasudeva as he is denied his father's lap (uttanpada) by his stepmother, Suruchi. Suruchi asked him instead to go and ask the Lord himself for that privilege.

Dhruv proceeded to the jungle and meditated for months. Despite being dissuaded by Narada, he was determined to seek the Lord. Finally, the Lord appeared. Moved by Dhruv's steadfastness and penance, He granted the boon and the position of a celestial body. It is believed that Dhruv sits in the lap of God; so, he is beyond any change and is constant. Dhruv is blessed with being untouched even during *maha pralaya* (great dissolution).

A beautiful allegory indeed for people stepping into a relationship, this universal story befits numerous types of partnerships where mutual dependency, guidance, growth, integrity, and equity form the foundation for a sustainable and evolved relationship.

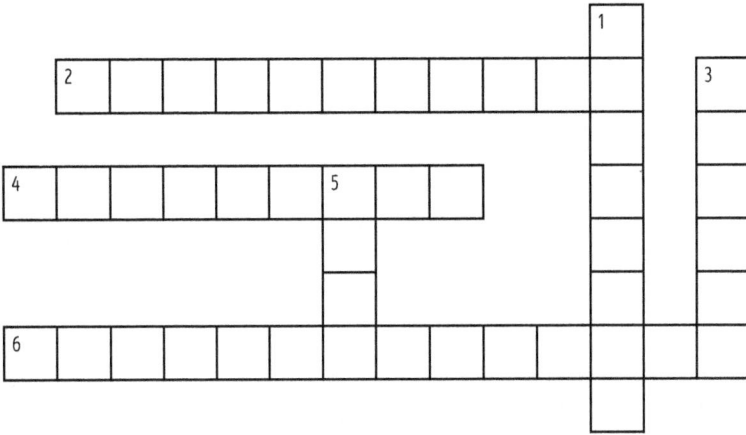

ACROSS

2 The Kshatriya who became a Brahmin and is also referred to as Raj Rishi or Brahma Raj

4 The only rishi wife of the Saptarshi wives whom Swaha could not impersonate to entice Agni

6 The Sanskrit treatise on Indian astronomy that describes rules to calculate planetary motion

DOWN

1 Rishi Vashishtha's cow, which was desired by Vishwamitra

3 The star that has, since ancient times, guided seafarers and travelers in determining their direction relative to the star's position in the sky

5 The Purana revealed by Agni to Sage Vashishtha

21

The power of solitude:
Save it for the last

Hinduism teaches life management through the *ashram* system—the journey of the mind from outside to inside. As a religious philosophy, Hinduism encourages self-experience and avoids a dogmatic approach. Seers and philosophers extolled the expansive experiential living that the *ashram* system offers. There are four *ashrams* in this system: *brahmacharya, grihastha, vanaprastha,* and *sanyasa.*

Brahmacharya Ashram: The student stage, characterized by obedience and discipline. The primary objective is to gain knowledge and develop various skills. This period typically spans from the age of 12 to 25 years.

Grihastha Ashram: The householder stage, where one takes on the primary responsibilities of family, marriage, procreation, and economic activities. This phase is generally considered to last from the age of 25 to 50 years.

Vanaprastha Ashram: The forest-dweller stage, where one gradually withdraws from material pursuits and practices asceticism, yoga, and meditation. This period is understood to extend from the age of 50 to 75 years.

Sanyasa Ashram: The renunciate stage, where one relinquishes all attachments to material possessions, family, name, and fame, choosing to live as an ascetic. This phase is believed to last from the age of 75 to 100 years or until death.

Even modern life coaches and spiritual gurus focus on experiential living as the best way to live fully. As a way of life, Hinduism suggests various measures to stay in harmony within and with the outside world and offers various preparatory tools for life management. One such preparatory tool is *ekant* or solitude. It is a powerful tool for self-awareness and acquiring true knowledge. *Ekantin,* or the person practicing *ekant,* is highly respected in Hindu religious and philosophical history. The Sanskrit word *ekantin* is translated as "devoted to one object only." *Ekantin* is highly revered in the Vaishnava sect of Hinduism.

To stay in isolation is a positive attribute; it is an idea of completeness within. A person practicing *ekant* internalizes knowledge that they have gathered through the scriptures or in the company of great sages. A person involved in acquiring deep knowledge should practice solitude to internalize the information they have gathered and process it into knowledge.

However, solitude is perceived differently by different people. For some, it is the absence of people and society, a negative state of isolation. We seek people and society to avoid solitude. If we have a problem with solitude, then it means that deep within, we have a problem with ourselves, with our thoughts. For some, solitude means quality time with oneself. Staying happy in solitude means we have started the inner journey. The idea of solitude is broad, from the perception of absence to the perception of self-presence.

To practice solitude is a strength in Hinduism. Two significant milestones of *ashram dharma* — *sanyasa ashram* and *vanaprastha ashram* — the annual spiritual renewal and cleansing ritual, *kalpwaas*, and *maun vrat* or the vow of silence, are practices that embrace the benefits of solitude. The practice of solitude is so integral and prescribed in the Hindu way of life that there is even a specific term — *ekantin* — for a person practicing silence and solitude. *Ekantin* is an influential person who has started their inner journey and is in harmony with their inner world.

Wise gurus, scholars, and sages advocated *ekantwaas* as essential to manage and prepare for the *sanyasa* stage. We cannot control the end of this physical body, so it is wise to accept and prepare for what we cannot control. The practice of solitude or *ekantwaas* is vital in this regard. *Ekantwaas* helps in practicing non-attachment to proceed to *vanaprastha* and *sanyasa*. Also, brief periods of *ekantwaas* were advocated as a method of repentance or *prayashchit* as people introspected on their actions when they were in solitude. Not reserved only for the third or fourth stages of life (*vanaprastha* or *sanyasa*), such practices were also advocated annually for cleansing and strengthening the mind. People practiced *maun vrat* (vow of silence) for a day, week, month, or year. Similarly, there were annual congregations of people at Prayagraj — *kalpwaas* — for a period of time.

In the Mahabharata, after the Kurukshetra war, the righteous Vidura was disturbed. He felt helpless at having been unable to stop the considerable loss of human life, including the lives of his relatives. At the same time, he felt guilty for being party to this bloodshed. Troubled by his actions and thoughts, he left the kingdom and wandered across the country. He stayed in solitude for days, practicing yoga and *yagna*. He remained in the company of the great sage Maitreya for some time and learned the secret knowledge of the self. He practiced solitude to internalize the knowledge he had gathered from Maitreya and other sages.

Vidura returned to Kurukshetra after several years of practicing solitude and traveling to sacred places. He looked calm and at peace. He shared his experiences with the royal family. However, he noticed that Dhritarashtra was deep in sorrow. Observing Dhritarashtra's sadness and distress despite his life of comfort and respect, it became evident to Vidura that his brother struggled to reconcile with his own inaction during the war. Dhritarashtra recognized that his support for Duryodhana's unethical ambitions and greed ultimately resulted in the loss of all his sons. Though Dhritarashtra could have acted to stop Duryodhana, he chose to remain silent. Now, he found himself unable to escape the anguish stemming from his past decisions. Vidura knew that Dhritarashtra was overwhelmed with guilt. He suggested that Dhritarashtra shun the life of comfort in the palace and move to the company of great sages, studying the Vedas at the bank of a sacred river and practicing *yagna* and yoga in solitude to gain relief from his mental agony.

After listening to Vidura's experiences, Dhritarashtra was in two minds about going into *vanaprastha* or continuing to stay in the palace. Yudhisthira, however, was not willing to let his uncle go. It was only after the guidance of the wise sage, Vyasa that Yudhisthira agreed to let his uncle go. Vyasa said, "O Yudhisthira, let the old King follow the royal path of the sages retiring to the woods. This is the highest duty of royal sages. According to the scriptures, they should die either in battle or in the woods." Sage Vyasa and wise Vidura knew that Dhritarashtra must practice penance for his wrongdoings and accept *vanaprastha ashram* to be in harmony and prepare for a glorious migration to the other world.

The practice of penance is highly valued in the Indian system. As action or *karma* is central to Hinduism, so is penance or *prayashchit* for our intentional or unintentional wrong actions.

Since there is no escape from *karma*, all the prescribed paths at the end lead to penance or *prayashchit*. A person practicing penance can act in various ways, such as accepting their misdeeds, engaging in charitable acts, fasting, going on pilgrimages, bathing in sacred waters, changing their lifestyle by residing in the forest or on the banks of a holy river, staying in the company of great sages, and meditating in solitude.

Vidura convinced Dhritarashtra that he must practice penance for his wrongdoings. He must repay through penance for his inaction when he needed to act. Inaction is as big a sin as intentional wrong actions. Vidura told Dhritarashtra that he and his sons tried to kill the Pandavas and forced immense suffering on them and Draupadi, but the Pandavas and Draupadi had ensured that Dhritarashtra and his wife spent the rest of their days in comfort and luxury. Now, it was time for Dhristrashtra to leave this royal comfort, proceed to the woods, stay in the company of great sages, and practice his inner journey.

Gandhari, Sanjay, and Vidura decided to accompany Dhritarashtra to the forest. Parting with their beloved uncle and seniors was sad for the royal clan and the Pandavas. But alas, who could ever fight destiny? The Pandavas were further saddened when Kunti, their beloved mother, decided to proceed to the banks of the sacred river to practice detachment

and penance along with Dhritarashtra and Gandhari. With her sons, their wives, and her grandchildren settled in the royal life, she felt it was the right time to proceed to *vanaprastha ashram*.

Though everyone tried to convince Kunti to stay in royal comfort because she had struggled hard in the past and her time had arrived now, she was firm in her resolve. She did not want to waste her life enjoying the fruits of the sovereignty that her virtuous children had earned. Her duty was over. She had been with her children when they had needed her most in difficult times, but she now wanted to gain merit through meditation and *yagna* while dwelling in the forest.

At the dawn of the next day, Dhritarashtra, Gandhari, Kunti, Sanjay, and Vidura proceeded to the city's outskirts to embark on their inner journey. After a few days of traveling, they reached the banks of the Bhagirathi at a place called *saptastrota*, where the river divided into seven streams.

They met the great sage Satyupa and stayed with him, bathing in the sacred waters and practicing yoga, meditation, and *yagna* Satyupa, the famous king of the Kekayas, had handed over the kingdom to his son and proceeded to the forest to celebrate the next stage of his life like a true royal.

To summarize, the journey starts from outward expression to inward realization, and the last two phases of *ashram dharma* help to progressively achieve inner realization. *Vanaprastha* and *sanyasa ashram* help in the gradual withdrawal from worldly obligations for a peaceful migration to the other world. Solitude has the power to aid our progress in inward realization, which is a prelude to peaceful migration to the other world.

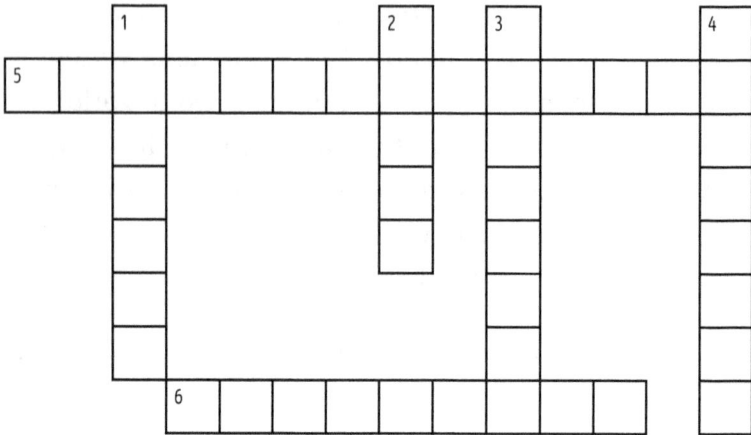

ACROSS

5 The teaching "*Brahma satya jagan mithya jivo Brahmaiva na aparah*" was given by _ _ _ _.

6 The god to whom one of the *chaar dhaam*, in Puri (East India), is dedicated

DOWN

1 The annual practice of Hindu devotees staying on the banks of Sangam from the 11th day of the month of Paush to the 12th day of the month of Magh

2 One of the three *gunas* in Samkhya philosophy

3 Commonly known as the school of Indian Materialism

4 Mayapuri is the ancient name of this famous *tirtha sthaan* or holy place

22

When uncertainty looms like a shadow, let truth be your guiding light: Jabala to Satyakama

In today's world, where uncertainty is widespread, a piece of timeless wisdom stands out: "When uncertainty looms like a shadow, let truth be your guiding light. It not only pierces the darkness of doubt but also paves the way forward with clarity."

This wisdom, rooted in the essence of truth, has been a central theme in the Vedas and Upanishads. *Satya* (truth), as it is known, holds intrinsic value, shining independently without reliance on external factors. Much like *dharma* protects its upholders, truth guides and shelters those who seek its refuge and believe in its power.

The intrinsic value of *satya* does not seek validation; it possesses its own light that shines brightly on seekers and beholders of truth. This is evident in the story of Satyakama, a young and curious seeker with a thirst for knowledge who embarked on a journey of

self-discovery. A self-starter, he decided to practice
brahmacharya under the guidance of a revered
guru. He had heard much about Sage Hiridrumata
Gautama and decided to pursue his *brahmacharya*
under his guidance.

Once he was sure about his decision, he declared
his intention to his mother, Jabala, a single parent.

Jabala was happy that her son was self-motivated
to seek the truth. She knew that it was self-
motivation, along with personal desire, that would
lead to the acquisition of knowledge and growth.
Jabala, delighted by her son's self-motivation, faced
an unexpected question. Satyakama asked her to
reveal the details of his lineage, including his father
and family. It was a norm that the presiding guru
would ask the student's lineage before accepting him
into *brahmacharya*. After a few moments of anxiety,

weakness, and contemplation, Jabala decided to embrace the truth, disclosing that Satyakama's lineage was unknown as, in her youth, she had traveled to various places and served many men. She told her son, "You can be known by my name, so introduce yourself as Jabala Satyakama."

Undeterred, Satyakama, now Jabala Satyakama, sought his mother's blessings and set off for Rishi Gautama's *ashram*. Upon reaching the *ashram*, Satyakama met Rishi Gautama, greeted him, and told him the purpose of his visit. Gautama, as expected, asked him about his lineage. Satyakama truthfully narrated his story, announcing himself as Jabala Satyakama, son of Jabala.

In this luminous moment of honesty, Gautama identified Satyakama's strong character and accepted him as a student. Gautama, through his experience and wisdom, knew that no ordinary person could speak this truth unfettered, so Satyakama was fit to be accepted as his pupil. Initiated into *brahmacharya* by the revered Sage Gautama, Jabala Satyakama started his profound learning journey. Later, Satyakama became a celebrated sage, and one of the important ancient texts, Jabala Upanishad, was named after him.

Truth or *satya* has been one of the core themes of Indian scriptures, and there have been various descriptions of *sat* or *satya*. The stories in these scriptures narrate the power of *satya* and explain how adhering to the truth is the same as divine reverence. Even the nirguna Brahman, the formless ultimate reality, is described as *sat* (truth), *chitta* (consciousness), and *anand* (bliss).

In the Mundaka Upanishad, a verse echoes, "सत्यमेव जयते नानृतं (3.1.6)," interpreted as "Truth alone triumphs, not falsehood" or "Truth ultimately prevails, not falsehood." This verse upholds the sanctity and strength of truth, motivating people to choose truth over falsehood in every situation. For those seeking knowledge and self-growth, speaking the truth is not just a requirement but a foundational principle. The Taittiriya Upanishad emphasizes this, urging individuals to speak the truth, practice righteousness, and not be lazy in self-study.

In his Yoga Sutras, Patanjali declares that when one is firmly established in speaking the truth, the fruits of action become subservient. In the Yoga Sutras, *satya* is one of the five *yamas*, or virtuous restraints, along with *ahimsa* (restraint from violence or injury to any living being), *asteya* (restraint from stealing), *brahmacharya* (celibacy or restraint from sexually cheating on one's partner), and *aparigraha* (restraint from covetousness and craving). *Satya* is a restraint from falsehood not only in one's words (speech or writing) but also in one's actions (body) and mind (feelings or thoughts).

The Sikh gurus also place truth (*sat*) at the forefront of the five virtues: *sat* or truth, *daya* or compassion, *santokh* or satisfaction, *pyaar* or love, and *nimrata* or humility. One of the famous Gurbanis says, "Those who do not have the assets of truth—how can they find peace?"

Satya is also one of the five vows described in the Jain Agamas, the others being *ahimsa* (non-violence), *asteya* (not stealing), *brahmacharya* (chastity), and *aparigraha* (non-possessiveness). The four noble truths of Buddhism talk about accepting the truths (*satya*) of life: suffering, the cause of suffering, the end of suffering, and the path leading to its end.

This story of Jabala Satyakama unveils profound truths in many ways. Jabala's decision to embrace the truth liberates her from the fear of her past, thus exemplifying the saying "Truth liberates." The story challenges societal norms, establishing that a mother's name suffices to introduce the child's lineage, advocating for equal recognition of women and respect for single mothers. It is a timeless lesson for parents to support their children truthfully and for mentors to identify pupils based on their character and values, laying a foundation rooted in authenticity.

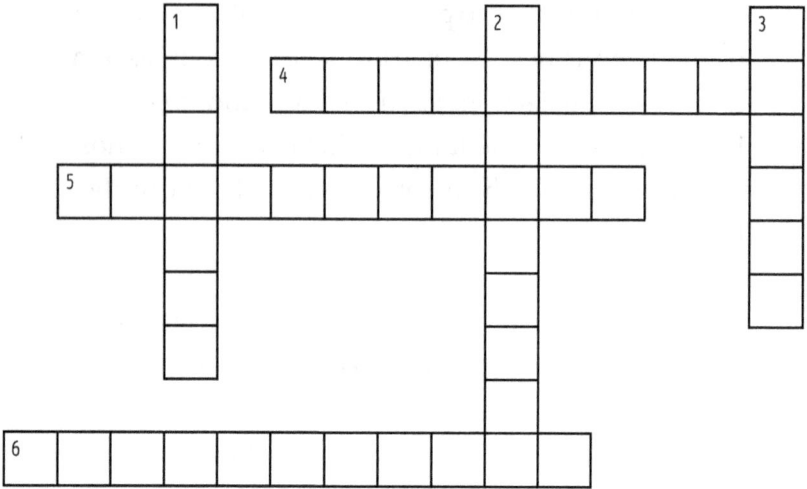

ACROSS

4 One of the five *yamas* (virtuous restraints) of Yoga Sutra

5 Apart from Bhagavadgita and Upanishad, which is the third canonical text which constitutes *prasathantrayi*

6 Earliest source of Hindu law

DOWN

1 Another name for Uttara Mimamsa school of *astika* tradition of Hindu philosophy

2 The number of *yoginis* depicted in one of the famous *yogini* temples of Khajuraho

3 The *ashram dharma* after *vanaprastha ashram*

Afterword

In compiling this collection of short stories from the the Vedas, Upanishads, Ramayana, Mahabharata, and Puranas, my goal was not to create an academic anthology but to present these timeless tales in a way that is simple for modern readers to grasp. Each story distills the essence of its characters and their challenging situations, communicating strong motivation, inspiration, and learning.

Every character in these stories — Yudhisthira, Yuyutsu, Shikhandi, Draupadi, Kubera, Indra, Nala, Damayanti, Sulabha, Jabala, Kevat, and others — offers valuable insights that encourage us to think beyond our present circumstances to create a brighter future.

As an author, the challenge was to make these profound narratives accessible to today's readers. One approach could have been to delve deeply into the life cycle of each character, offering a comprehensive exploration of their journeys. However, I chose to create short stories to cater to readers who seek meaningful engagement without the time commitment required for longer texts. This approach also serves those eager to gain insights from a variety of characters and situations across multiple scriptures.

This book is designed to meet the needs of new-age readers — those with limited time and those eager for broad exposure to scriptural wisdom. Apart from general readers interested in this genre, educators from primary to higher education, keen on implementing universal human values sessions in their campuses, will find this collection particularly useful, as will trainers seeking enriching content for storytelling sessions.

While developing each story, I was often intrigued by the myriad possibilities and moral dilemmas faced by the characters. These tales transport readers to different social setups, allowing them to imagine themselves in similar situations and derive personal meaning from these ancient narratives. A recurring thought was: How would these stories have changed if the characters had made different choices? Would the moral and ethical outcomes, leadership lessons, decision-making principles, and conflict resolution strategies have remained the same?

For instance, if Yudhisthira had not been aware

of the prophecy by Narada and Ved Vyasa, would he still have accepted the invitation to play the game of dice? And if he had played without the awareness of the prophecy, then would there have been any justification for staking his brothers, his wife, and the entire treasury of his kingdom? Even knowing the prophecy, could he have acted differently?

Consider Yuyutsu, who chose to side with the Pandavas at the last moment. Was saving his life in the war the only outcome of this decision, or did it have a larger impact? How would the world of today view Yuyutsu — a smart opportunist or a person who corrected himself at the last moment?

Various stories leave readers pondering whether the same beliefs about human relationships still hold true. Was Draupadi justified in advising Satyabhama on gaining her husbands' trust? Was her strong relationship with her husbands part of her destiny or the result of her efforts? Does relationship management still work on these principles? I found the answers to be largely affirmative, with perhaps some necessary adjustments for our evolving times.

Yudhisthira's selfless act of asking for the Akshay Patra to feed Brahmins, instead of immediate relief from his exile, speaks volumes about his character. Did he accept his fate as a consequence of his choices? Did this character of endurance make him stronger or merely delay his justice?

Lord Indra's handling of the issue between Brahaspati, Tara, and Chandra raises questions about the superiority of the *dharma* of a wife over that of a lover. Did Indra believe in the superiority of the *dharma* of a wife, or were his decisions likely influenced by the fear of Brahaspati's wrath? These chapters can provoke endless discussions where each perspective is justified by its own set of reasons.

Dealing with ego, as showcased by Indra, and the importance of mentorship, as exemplified by Uddalaka guiding Shvetketu, highlight lessons still relevant today. What fate would Shvetketu have met without his father's intervention? The importance of guidance and mentorship remains as crucial today as it was in antiquity.

The humor of the humble boatman in the Ramayana shows the value of levity and devotion. Would he have managed to seek Lord Rama's blessing without his wit? Krishna's strategic role in Subhadra's abduction illustrates the necessity of long-term planning and strategy, akin to modern principles of 360-degree feedback and comprehensive planning.

The redemption in Nala and Damayanti's story parallels the transformative journey of Kubera, reminding us that barriers exist only in our minds. Kubera's rise from demon king to a god worshipped by Hindus, Jains, and Buddhists for thousands of years is an inspiring testament to the power of transformation.

The story of Prajapati's eternal teachings to his descendants urges us to understand the true intent behind communication, be it with parents, family, friends, teachers, students, or colleagues. As you progressed through these stories, I hope you gained fresh perspectives on navigating your interaction with others.

Jabala and Sulabha, contrasting characters who champion the power of truth, show that challenging societal norms can come from any stratum. Jabala, despite her humble background, and Sulabha, from a scholarly elite class, both made significant marks in their eras. These women, along with Draupadi, Arundhati, and Lopamudra, existed millennia ago, yet their courage and resilience inspire contemporary youth.

Practices mentioned in the book, like solitude, selfless charity, gratitude, and awareness of our debts, are important even today. Writing about the philosophy behind *pitripaksha*, I realized that repaying societal and familial debts addresses broader social concerns, like caring for the environment and supporting elders, and also helps to support scholars who would ultimately contribute in the knowledge economy of the modern world.

My hope is that this book piques readers'

interest in the endless and eternal relevance of these scriptures, showing that ancient challenges and tribulations can still inspire and guide the modern quest for a meaningful life.

May these stories help you see beyond the immediate and inspire you to cultivate wisdom, resilience, and compassion in your journey.

Crossword Solutions

1 Yudhisthira trapped in a prophecy:
Some answers need a deeper search

¹D							²R	
H			³V	I	D	U	R	
A			A				K	
U		⁴O	N	E			M	
M			A				I	
Y							N	
⁵S	A	T	Y	A	V	A	T	I

ACROSS

3 Brother of Dhritarashtra and Pandu

4 The number of years for Pandavas to stay in disguise (*agyatvaas*) after they lost the dice game

5 Stepmother of Bhishma Pitamah

DOWN

1 Guru Bhakt Aruni was the disciple of this famous rishi

2 Whose marriage with Krishna was the cause of enmity between Shishupala and Krishna?

3 The Parva of the Mahabharata that describes the forest exile period of the Pandavas

2 Tomorrow is another day:
Yuyutsu rose to Dharma

									¹K
				²S		³K			R
⁴D	E	V	A	V	R	A	T	A	I
				N		R			P
⁵P	A	N	C	H	A	J	A	N	Y	A
				A					
		⁶Y	U	Y	U	T	S	U	

ACROSS

4   Another name for Bhishma Pitamah

5   Name given to Krishna's conch

6   Son of Dhritarashtra and Sugadha

DOWN

1   The acharya who was a great archer and teacher of both the Pandavas and the Kauravas. He was adopted by King Shantanu as an infant

2   Dhritarashtra's charioteer who had the gift of seeing things at long distance

3   Kunti's son and the Pandavas' half-brother who fought on the Kauravas' side in the Kurukshetra war

3 Untangling Happiness:
Yajnavalkya and Maitreyi

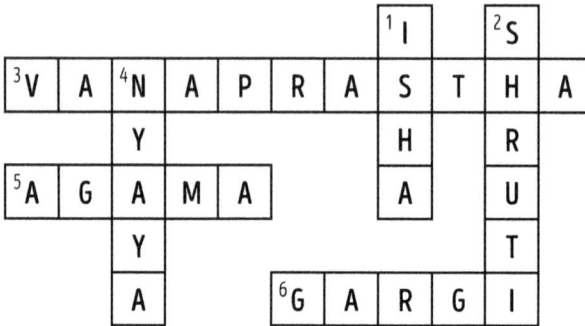

							¹I		²S	
³V	A	⁴N	A	P	R	A	S	T	H	A
		Y					H		R	
⁵A	G	A	M	A			A		U	
		Y							T	
		A			⁶G	A	R	G	I	

ACROSS

3 The *ashram dharma* which was a transition stage to prepare for the final renunciation and places emphasis on pursuing *moksha*

5 The *shastra* (text) that clarifies and explains the methodology of worship

6 Another famous female Veda scholar during Maitreyi's time

DOWN

1 So'hamasmi (सोहमस्मि), the prayer mantra meaning "I am He" or "Even when I pray to You, I am You" is from which Upanishad?

2 Manusmriti is a Smriti, whereas the Vedas are classified as _ _ _ _ _

4 The school of Indian philosophy that discusses logic and epistemology in detail

4 *Pitripaksha:*
Everyone has a debt to repay

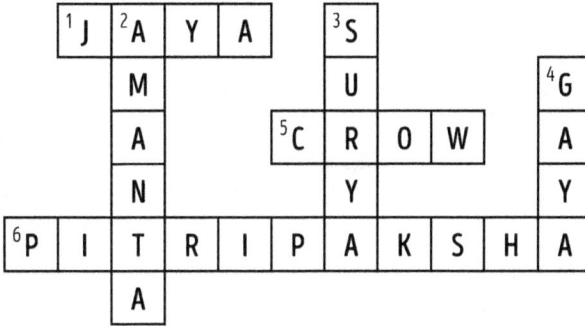

	¹J	²A	Y	A		³S				⁴G
		M				U				G
		A		⁵C	R	O	W			A
		N			Y					Y
⁶P	I	T	R	I	P	A	K	S	H	A
		A								

ACROSS

1 One of the gatekeepers of Vaikuntha

5 This bird is believed to be the messenger of our ancestors

6 The annual period when *shraadh* is performed for our ancestors

DOWN

2 What is the Hindu lunar calendar system in which the lunar month ends with *amavasya* called?

3 Yamaraj's father

4 One of the important centers of *shraadh* in India

5 The woman who lit her lamp:
The dialogue between Janak and Sulabha

¹J										²S	
³P	A	N	C	H	A	S	H	I	K	H	A
A	N									M	
⁴M	A	N	U	S	M	R	⁵I	T	I	K	
A	K					S				H	
	⁶S	U	L	A	B	H	A			Y	
					A					A	

ACROSS

3 Janak's guru

4 Popular or common name of Manav Dharma Shastra

6 The *rishika* who won in a philosophical debate with King Janak

DOWN

1 Ruler of Mithila

2 The school of Indian philosophy that introduced the concept of the world being the interplay of *purusha* and *prakriti*

5 The other prominent Upanishad, along with the Brihadaranyaka Upanishad, that is associated with the Yajurveda

6 Akshay Patra:
Redefining our *patra* of values

```
                    ¹S              ²F              ³J
              ⁴D    U    R    Y    O    D    H    A    N
                    R              U                   I
                    Y              R                   N
    ⁵K    A    M    Y    A    K    A                   I
                                                       S
    ⁶P    U    R    U    S    H    O    T    T    A    M
```

ACROSS

4 Suyodhan's common name in the Mahabharata

5 The forest where the Pandavas stayed at the start of their exile period

6 Another name for *adhik maas* (month)

DOWN

1 The god who gave Akshay Patra to Yudhisthira

2 The total number of *yugas* according to Hinduism

3 The religion that propounds the belief in *chaturvidha* of *anna daan, abhay daan, aushadha daan,* and *gyaan daan*

7 Subhadra haran:
Serendipity or strategy?

	¹P		²C	H	I	T	R	³A	S	E	N	A
	U							R				
	R		⁴F					J				
	O		O					U				
	C		U					N				
⁵C	H	I	T	R	A	V	A	H	A	N	A	
	A											
⁶I	N	D	R	A	P	R	A	S	T	H	A	
	A											

ACROSS

2 Musician at Indra's palace who taught Arjuna the music of the celestials

5 The king of Manipur and father of Princess Chitrangada—one of Arjuna's wives

6 The name given to the Pandavas' capital at Khandavaprastha

DOWN

1 Duryodhana's trusted aide, who was given the task of making the lakshagriha to kill the Pandavas in the fire

3 The Pandava brother who was ambidextrous

4 The total number of Arjuna's wives, including Draupadi

8 Amba reborn as Shikhandi:
Gender fluidity for a purpose

					¹D					
²S					R					
A		³D	E	V	A	V	R	A	T	⁴A
L					U					M
V					P					B
⁵S	A	T	Y	A	V	A	T	I		A
					D					
⁶S	A	T	Y	A	J	I	T			

ACROSS

3 Bhishma Pitamah's childhood name

5 Vichitravirya's mother

6 The commander-in-chief of the Panchala army in King Drupada's reign; popularly known as Chitraratha in the Mahabharata

DOWN

1 Shikhandi's sister

2 The king who tried to counter Bhishma's attempt to kidnap the three sisters—Amba, Ambika, and Ambalika—from their swayamvar

4 One of the three princesses abducted by Bhishma for marriage to his half-brother, Vichitravirya

9 Ahankara:
Guard it tight to get it right!

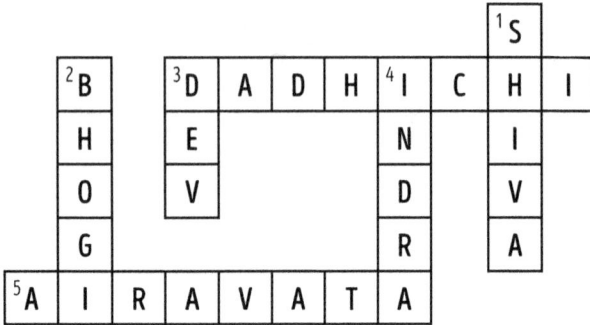

								¹S	
²B		³D	A	D	H	⁴I	C	H	I
H		E				N		I	
O		V				D		V	
G						R		A	
⁵A	I	R	A	V	A	T	A		

ACROSS
3 The great sage who contributed his bones to make the weapon, *vajrayuddha*, to defeat the demon Vritta

5 Indra's elephant

DOWN
1 Ravana was the devout follower of this god

2 The name of the festival celebrated in Telangana, Andhra Pradesh, Tamil Nadu, and Karnataka to worship Lord Indra, the god of rains and clouds, to bring good rain, harvest, and prosperity

3 In Varanasi, this Deepavali is celebrated on Kartik Purnima to mark the killing of the demon Tripurasur by Lord Shiva

4 A prominent Rigvedic god

10 Nala and Damayanti:
The story which redeemed Yudhisthira

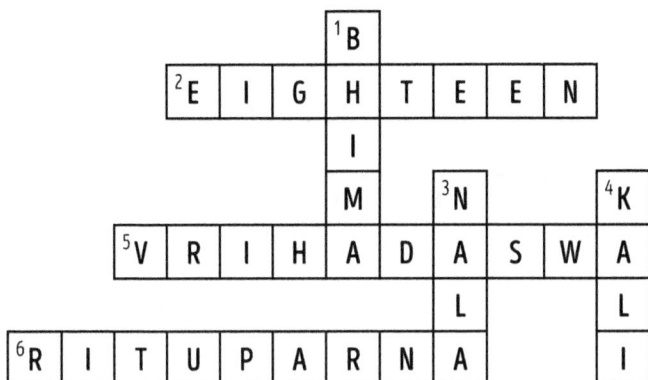

		¹B					

Across 2: ²E I G H T E E N

Down 1: B H I M A L A

Across 5: ⁵V R I H A D A S W A

Down 3: N A L A

Down 4: ⁴K A L I

Across 6: ⁶R I T U P A R N A

ACROSS

2 The total number of Parvas in the Mahabharata

5 The sage who narrated the story of Nala and Damayanti to Yudhisthira

6 After losing the game of dice, Nala, in disguise, became a charioteer to this king

DOWN

1 Damayanti's father

3 Damayanti's husband, known for his great cooking skills

4 The demon who convinced Nala to play a game of dice with his brother, Pushkara, in which Nala lost everything he had

11 Chandra:
The retainer of our mind loses his heart

	¹A									

Across row: ²T W E N T Y S E V E N

³B R I H A S P A T ⁴I

⁵B U D D H A (with N, R in column 4 reading INDRA down)

⁶S H U K R A C H A R Y A

ACROSS

2 The total number of wives Chandra is believed to have

3 The chief priest of the gods

5 Devi Tara and Lord Chandra's love-child

6 The guru or priest of the demons

DOWN

1 Chandra's father and a famous sage

4 The god who took steps to resolve the conflict between Chandra and Brahaspati

12 Lopamudra and Agastya:
Exploring the relationship

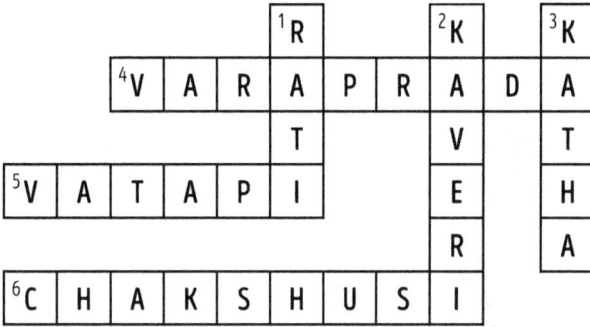

		¹R				²K		³K
⁴V	A	R	A	P	R	A	D	A
		T				V		T
⁵V	A	T	A	P	I		E		H
						R		A
⁶C	H	A	K	S	H	U	S	I

ACROSS

4 Another name for Lopamudra

5 Atapi's demon brother, who was digested by Rishi Agastya

6 The art of illusion exclusively known to the gandharvas, which was imparted to Arjuna after he defeated a Gandharva

DOWN

1 Goddess of love

2 The river in South India associated with Lopamudra

3 The Upanishad that contains the famous dialogue between Nachiketa and Yamaraj

13 Prajapati's eternal teaching:
Da... Da... Da..

```
                                    ¹P
        ²S                           U
         A       ³T      ⁴D  A  K  S  H  A
         T        W       E           H
         T        E       M           K
         V        L       O           A
⁵D  H  A  N  V  A  N  T  A  R  I
                  E       S
```

ACROSS

4 One of the Prajapatis
5 The physician of the gods (devas)

DOWN

1 A city in India that is famous for its Brahma Temple and the annual camel festival in the month of Kartik
2 One of the three *gunas*, associated with goodness, purity, and peace
3 The number of years after which Purna Kumbh is celebrated
4 The descendants of Prajapati who understood his teaching to mean "practice compassion"

14 Agni:
Balancing it right

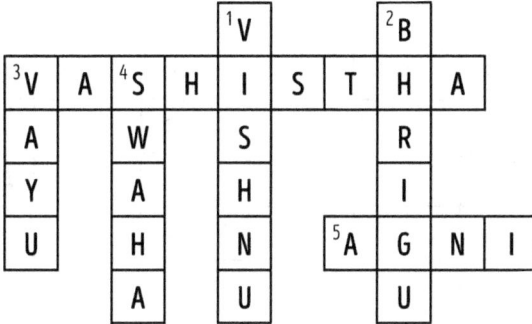

```
                    ¹V            ²B
³V   A   ⁴S   H    I    S    T    H    A
A        W        S              R
Y        A        H              I
U        H        N        ⁵A    G    N    I
         A        U              U
```

ACROSS

3 The sage to whom Agni revealed the nature of Brahman which was written in Agni Puran by Ved Vyas

5 The god who is believed to stay permanently in the kingdom of Mahishmati

DOWN

1 The Hindu god who is believed to sleep (Yog Nidra) for four months during which no auspicious activities are planned

2 Rishi who cursed Agni to become devourer of all things in the world

3 One of the Panchabhutas along with Agni

4 Daksha's daughter and Agni's wife

15 Uddalaka to Shvetketu:
Humble heroes have always won the war

```
                                          ¹M
  ²T  A   T   T   V   A  ³M   A   S    I
                          A            M
   ⁴D                     Y            A
 ⁵A   I   T   A   R   E   Y   A        M
   T                                  S
   I          ⁶M   A   N   D   U   K   Y   A
```

ACROSS

2   The famous mahavakya from Chandogya Upanishad

5   The famous Mahavakya "prajnanam Brahman" meaning "consciousness is the absolute (Brahman)" is from which upanishad

6   Shortest Upanishad

DOWN

1   One of the six major astik (thesitic) schools of Vedic philosophy founded by Jaimini

3   The face or veil that creates the cosmic illusion, presenting phenomenal world to the real according to Advaita Vedanta

4   Hiranyakashipu's mother

16 Look here, look there, you will find them everywhere: Dikpala guarding us all the way

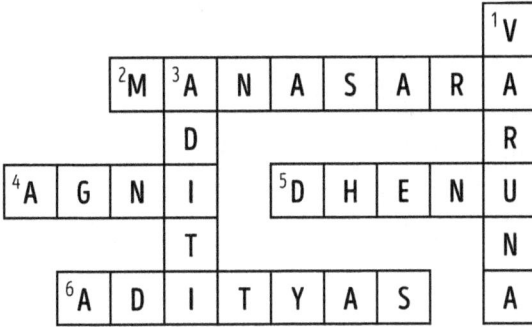

								¹V
	²M	³A	N	A	S	A	R	A
		D						R
⁴A	G	N	I		⁵D	H	E	N	U
		T						N
	⁶A	D	I	T	Y	A	S	A

ACROSS

2 Sanskrit treatise on ancient Indian architecture and design

4 The guardian of the southeast direction

5 Kamadhenu's daughter who guards the north direction

6 One common name for these 12 gods: Vivasvan, Aryaman, Tvashta, Savitr, Bhaga, Data, Mitra, Varuna, Amsa, Pushan, Indra, and Vishnu (Vamana form)

DOWN

1 The dikpala who rides a crocodile

3 Mother of the Adityas

17 The sagacious dialogue:
Lord Rama and Kevat

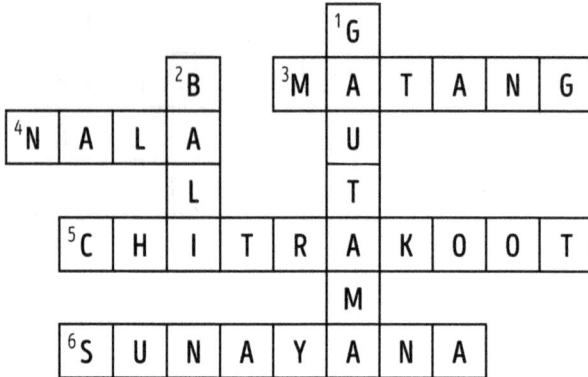

			¹G			
	²B	³M	A	T	A	N	G
⁴N	A	L	A	U		
		L	T			
⁵C	H	I	T	R	A	K	O	O	T
		M				
⁶S	U	N	A	Y	A	N	A

ACROSS

3 The sage who was Sabri's guru, and prophesied that Rama would visit her in the ashram one day

4 The architect of Ram Setu to Lanka , who is also known to be Lord Vishwakarma's son

5 The forest area where Rama, Lakshmana, and Sita spent the initial years of exile; the famous place where Bharata, upon hearing of Rama's exile, came to meet him and request him to return to Ayodhya

6 King Janak's wife and Sita's mother

DOWN

1 The famous sage who was Ahilya's husband and cursed her to turn into a stone

2 The demon king for whom Bali Pratipada is celebrated

18 Embracing impermanence:
Kubera's rise to divinity

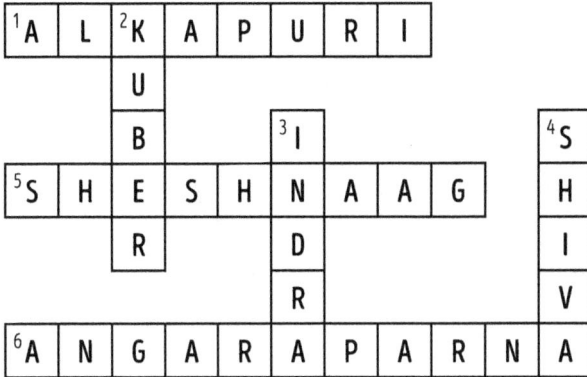

¹A	L	²K	A	P	U	R	I	
		U						
		B		³I				⁴S
⁵S	H	E	S	H	N	A	A	G	H
		R		D				I
				R				V
⁶A	N	G	A	R	A	P	A	R	N	A

ACROSS

1 The abode of Kubera
5 The serpent associated with Lord Vishnu
6 Kubera's friend, a gandharva, who stopped Arjuna from touching the waters of the Bhagirathi

DOWN

2 The god who is also known as Ekaksipingala, meaning one who has one yellow eye
3 The god who gifted Pushpak Vimana to Kubera
4 The god whose celestial bow is called Pinaka

19 Draupadi and Satyabhama's Conversation:
Quest for a blessed relationship

							¹G			
²S		³P	R	A	D	Y	U	M	N	A
H							D			
⁴S	A	T	R	A	J	I	T	A		
R							A			
A				⁵S	U	D	E	S	H	N	A
D							S			
	⁶S	A	T	Y	A	B	H	A	M	A

ACROSS

3 Kamdev's incarnation, born out of Krishna and one of his chief consorts, Rukmini

4 A Yadav king and Satyabhama's father

5 In one year of living in disguise, Draupadi became the hairdresser (*sairandhri*) to this queen

6 Lord Krishna's wife, who helped him fight against the demon Narkasur

DOWN

1 Arjuna's name because of his curly hair and because he had conquered sleep

2 One of the *purnimas* on which Lord Krishna is believed to have performed the famous *maharaas*

20 Partnering for life:
Starry tales from Arundhati-Vashishtha and Dhruv Tara

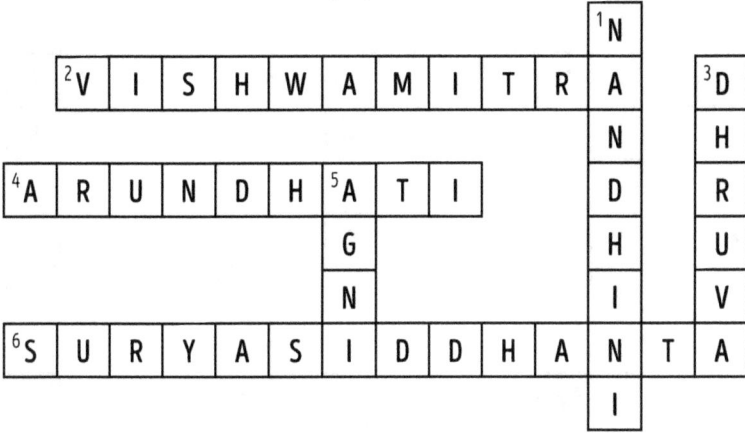

										¹N			³D
²V	I	S	H	W	A	M	I	T	R	A			H
										N			R
⁴A	R	U	N	D	H	⁵A	T	I		D			U
				G					H			V
				N					I			A
⁶S	U	R	Y	A	S	I	D	D	H	A	N	T	A
										I			

ACROSS

2 The Kshatriya who became a Brahmin and is also referred to as Raj Rishi or Brahma Raj

4 The only rishi wife of the Saptarshi wives whom Swaha could not impersonate to entice Agni

6 The Sanskrit treatise on Indian astronomy that describes rules to calculate planetary motion

DOWN

1 Rishi Vashishtha's cow, which was desired by Vishwamitra

3 The star that has, since ancient times, guided seafarers and travelers in determining their direction relative to the star's position in the sky

5 The Purana revealed by Agni to Sage Vashishtha

21 The power of solitude:
Save it for the last

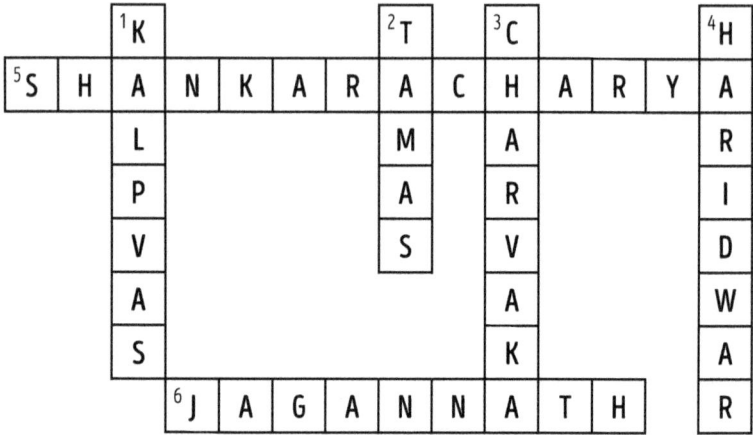

	¹K						²T		³C				⁴H
⁵S	H	A	N	K	A	R	A	C	H	A	R	Y	A
	L						M		A				R
	P						A		R				I
	V						S		V				D
	A								A				W
	S								K				A
		⁶J	A	G	A	N	N	A	T	H			R

ACROSS

5 The teaching "*Brahma satya jagan mithya jivo Brahmaiva na aparah*" was given by ＿＿＿＿.

6 The god to whom one of the *chaar dhaam*, in Puri (East India), is dedicated

DOWN

1 The annual practice of Hindu devotees staying on the banks of Sangam from the 11th day of the month of Paush to the 12th day of the month of Magh

2 One of the three *gunas* in Samkhya philosophy

3 Commonly known as the school of Indian Materialism

4 Mayapuri is the ancient name of this famous *tirtha sthaan* or holy place

22 When uncertainty looms like shadow, let truth be your guiding light:
Jabala to Satyakama

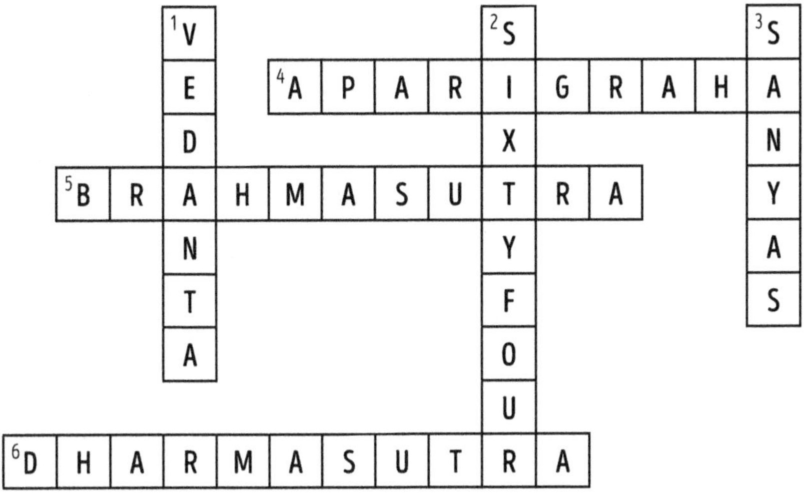
1 VEDANTA
2 SIXTYFOUR
3 SANYAS
4 APARIGRAHA
5 BRAHMASUTRA
6 DHARMASUTRA

ACROSS

4 One of the five *yamas* (virtuous restraints) of Yoga Sutra

5 Apart from the Bhagavad Gita and Upanishad, which is the third canonical text which constitutes *prasathantrayi*

6 Earliest source of Hindu law

DOWN

1 Another name for Uttara Mimamsa school of *astika* tradition of Hindu philosophy

2 The number of *yoginis* depicted in one of the famous *yogini* temples of Khajuraho

3 The *ashram dharma* after *vanaprastha*

Acknowledgements

My deepest gratitude to my parents for their persistent motivation and inspiration to seek a purpose beyond the routine.

To my loving husband, Rajesh, whose steadfast support and constant encouragement made the completion of this book possible.

To my lovely daughters, Kimaya and Sumaya, for being the sun of my life.

My bouquet of cherished relationships — my sister, brother, their better halves, my in-laws, and friends — who have kept me grounded with their love, affection, and simply by being there.

The editorial team at Jaico Publishing House for being a guiding light and showing me the way forward.

To the Almigty for making my life meaningful.

JAICO PUBLISHING HOUSE
Elevate Your Life. Transform Your World.

ESTABLISHED IN 1946, Jaico Publishing House is home to world-transforming authors such as Robin Sharma, Sadhguru, Osho, the Dalai Lama, Deepak Chopra, Eknath Easwaran, Paramhansa Yogananda, Devdutt Pattanaik, Radhakrishnan Pillai, Morgan Housel, Napoleon Hill, John Maxwell, Brian Tracy, and Stephen Hawking.

Our late founder Mr. Jaman Shah first established Jaico as a book distribution company. Sensing that independence was around the corner, he aptly named his company Jaico ('Jai' means victory in Hindi). In order to service the significant demand for affordable books in a developing nation, Mr. Shah initiated Jaico's own publications. Jaico was India's first publisher of paperback books in the English language.

While self-help; religion and philosophy; mind, body and spirit; and business titles form the cornerstone of our non-fiction list, we publish an exciting range of current affairs, history, biography, art and architecture, travel, and popular science books as well. Our renewed focus on popular fiction is evident in our new titles by a host of fresh young talent from India and abroad.

Jaico's translations division publishes select bestselling titles in over 10 regional languages including Gujarati, Hindi, Kannada, Malayalam, Marathi, Tamil, and Telugu. These include titles from renowned national and international authors like Sudha Murthy, Gaur Gopal Das, Swami Mukundananda, Jay Shetty, Simon Sinek, Ankur Warikoo and Jeff Keller.

Visit our Website

Boasting one of India's largest book distribution networks, Jaico has its headquarters in Mumbai, with branches in Ahmedabad, Bangalore, Chennai, Delhi, Hyderabad, and Kolkata. This network ensures that our books reach all parts of the country, both urban and rural.

www.ingramcontent.com/pod-product-compliance
Lightning Source LLC
Chambersburg PA
CBHW062056080426
42734CB00012B/2668